The Experience of Reality

Shankara's *Aparokshanubhuti*
for the Western World

Translated by Joseph Kloss

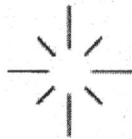

Not Two Press

Published by:

Not Two Press

Greer, South Carolina

www.nottwopress.com

ISBN 978-0-9794568-2-4

LCCN 2013902452

This book is dedicated to us;

to all of us.

CONTENTS

Preface   1

Introduction   5

Text   13

Text with Commentary   41

Afterword   109

Acknowledgements   115

Appendices   117

Preface

A friend prompted this preface by asking why anyone would want to produce another translation of such an old and obscure book.

The Crisis of Consciousness
Have we overslept?

After thousands of years of accelerating development, we humans are awakening to find ourselves hurtling toward an evolutionary precipice. Our momentum is such that we cannot immediately slow our pace and we can see that there are only moments left in which to change our direction. Our present trajectory is leading straight into environmental and socio-political calamity as natural resources are exhausted and ecosystems are destabilized under the weight of our prolonged short-sightedness. Our only reasonable response is to make a bold change of direction, to take another road.

Taking another road can lead us to a fighting chance for the continuation of life in general and our species in particular. A new direction also provides for the continued evolution of our individual and collective consciousness, which we have just begun to recognize as our defining characteristic.

Within our field of vision lie many new kinds of information that can help us determine the most prudent alternatives for changing our direction. If we are to endure, we must hasten to use this knowledge.

The knowledge that is available to us is at least threefold. First is the objective comprehension of our current global predicament and our collective willingness to concede the manifold crises that confront us. Many of these facts are not new, but we have ignored them for as long as we dare.

The Experience of Reality

Second is the new information arising from ongoing scientific inquiry into the nature of reality. This knowledge promises to revolutionize our understanding of matter and mind. We have recently accepted the fact that the universe is much larger, more massive, and more dynamic than we had thought, but we are just beginning to appreciate the implications of discoveries that point to an indivisible presence underlying all appearances, a field of 'something' which manifests as the material universe.

The third kind of knowledge can be classified as "new" even though it has been present among us for thousands of years. This new knowledge is called ancient wisdom.

The ancient wisdom traditions of the world are sources of a category of intelligence that addresses the fundamental realities of our existence. Historically, these insights have had little impact on our collective scientific world-view. The Western mindset had summarily rejected these "primitive" philosophies because they were dependent upon assertions that were unverifiable through accepted empirical methods. But technological acuity and the depth of our scientific inquiry have continued to evolve and now reveal new data regarding consciousness and the nature of the universe. In this new information we can hear echoes of the wisdom traditions.

At the same time that the pendulum of circumstances swings farther toward social, economic, and environmental chaos, there is, at the other end of the pendulum's arc, an unprecedented awakening taking place among human beings. This awakening arises from a source more fundamental than the simple recognition of the crisis of consciousness that is bringing us to the brink of calamity. Emerging among us is a most profound awareness that reflects the ancient affirmations of the wisdom traditions, a consciousness that sees beyond our earthly condition and can discern the very ground of our being.

This new awareness appears to be developing as a result of the momentum of our collective consciousness, which is manifesting for some as a renewed interest in the teachings of the ancient wisdom traditions. Whether our interest in heightened awareness is generated from sources ancient or contemporary, this pursuit can sometimes lead to the adoption of contemplative activities that are known to bring about transformations in consciousness, and can potentially lead to the experience of awakening.

Preface

Awakening, in this context, is defined as the *experience* of reality, a direct personal encounter with the unity of all things. This experience is accompanied by the certainty that each of us is an integral part of that oneness and that, ultimately, each of us *is* that oneness.

The wisdom teachers who have appeared throughout human history represent the leading edge of an evolutionary wave, the first examples of what is possible for us. Although instruction at this advanced level has been available for many centuries, most of us are unaware of its value or even its existence. Only recently have we begun to realize that we hunger for true sustenance. We have spent our lives feeding upon what lies at hand, and now find ourselves malnourished and unprepared for the impending crisis of consciousness that looms over our world.

This book presents the instructions of one of the world's great repositories of ancient wisdom teachings. Here we find a fitting example of the kind of knowledge that has been alive in the wisdom traditions for millennia. This "new information" has the potential to reveal fresh insights about the nature of reality and, ultimately, to cultivate within us the fertile ground of our own Being, from which we can reap the experience of Reality.

The Experience of Reality

Introduction

How can we think about reality? The word itself is so all-inclusive that our attempts to define it are instantly limited, both by our language and by our minds, which are necessarily a product of whatever reality is. It does not help that the words "reality" and "truth" invariably point toward one another with little else to help define them. Perhaps the best we can do is acknowledge that reality is the ultimate truth even though we cannot expect to know the entirety of that truth.

Our consideration of such an enormous topic must rely on the information we can bring together from what is already known. We can incorporate the observations of science and human history, the speculations of philosophy, the assertions of religion, and, in order to cover all the bases, we must include information gathered from metaphysical and mystical traditions. In addition to these resources, we should incorporate our own personal experience, including our intuition, to help us approach what is finally real and true.

To understand reality is the ultimate objective of human inquiry and the very meaning of wisdom. The search for this kind of understanding has intrigued humanity for millennia. Throughout our history there are reports of individuals able to penetrate the heights and depths of our existence and to directly experience levels of reality entirely beyond normal comprehension. Some of these men and women have attempted to describe their experience and a few have left instructions intended to help us discover this experience for ourselves. We often refer to this kind of guidance as "wisdom teachings."

The attempt to communicate the essence and meaning of wisdom is a major theme of many of the ancient writings that have survived to the present day. Among these early wisdom teachings, many of the most cogent examples have appeared in a corner of the ancient world called the Indus Valley, later identified as India and, since the middle of the 20th century, as Pakistan and India.

The Experience of Reality

We can better appreciate the significance of these early writings if we look briefly at the qualities of the culture that flourished in that region nearly five thousand years ago. [1]

It was not until the 20th century that archaeologists were aware of the existence of an ancient civilization in the Indus Valley. With its traceable origins in the early Stone Age, there was another group of human beings sharing the stage with Egypt, Mesopotamia, Sumer, and China in ancient times. There is even recent speculation that the population and organization of the Indus Valley actually predated these other civilizations. But whatever its chronology, it was a culture that demonstrated many intriguing qualities.

From 7000 BCE, communities in the Indus Valley grew in size and sophistication until, by 2800 to 2000 BCE, numerous cities and hundreds of towns had come into existence. Today the largest of these cities are identified as Harappa and Mohenjo-daro.

Although this civilization is thought to have disappeared as a result of prolonged drought, it left adequate archaeological evidence to suggest uncommon intelligence and advanced development.

The Indus Valley civilization is especially distinguished by the organization of daily life. Communities were laid out in grids with main streets oriented in the cardinal directions. The homes were permanent multi-room fired-brick dwellings. Unlike hierarchical societies, homes were all approximately the same size, with courtyards, wells, indoor bathing facilities, and toilets, all connected to a covered sewer system. There were standardized weights and measures, and evidence of effective medical and dental practice based upon a sophisticated knowledge of anatomy and physiology.

Especially thought-provoking is the absence of evidence of a centralized governing power during a time when all concurrent civilizations were controlled by kings, pharaohs, or emperors. In the cities of this unique culture there were neither palaces nor temples; the only large buildings were granaries and communal baths. Some archaeologists speculate that the communal baths may have had religious significance, as evidenced by the practice of ritual bathing in historical and contemporary Hinduism.

---

[1] Appendix A contains an informal bibliography and a list of websites that could be useful to anyone who wishes to learn more about the topics discussed in this introduction.

Introduction

The archaeological evidence indicates that a well-organized and arguably peaceful society existed in the Indus Valley during a period of human history in which peace was the exception. The available evidence is suggestive of at least the possibility of an egalitarian society which was a rarity among ancient cultures and remains so today.

Early on, the people of the Indus Valley recognized the Sun as a star and as the source of moonlight. They calculated the length of the year by 2500 BCE and identified the equinoxes. Over time, as this region came to be called India, the inhabitants proceeded to recognize the heliocentric nature of the solar system, predict eclipses, identify the planets, calculate the circumference of the earth, and explore the qualities of gravitation and light. They identified zero as a number and discovered the place value system, decimal number system, geometry, algebra, trigonometry, and a host of abstract mathematical concepts and formulae.

If the people who lived in this region during these early times had progressed to such advanced levels of development and knowledge of the physical world, what is the likelihood that their philosophical perspectives were similarly advanced? It is intriguing to imagine that philosophers of the Indus region fulfilled the speculative and theoretical pursuits that characterize philosophy as an inquiry into ultimate truth, and that, having achieved advanced levels of understanding, they continued the pursuit of truth into the direct experience of reality. Speculation of this sort is supported by the profundity of the ancient writings which have survived into the present day. An additional indicator of the presumed wisdom of this ancient culture is the discovery in the Indus Valley of the first known images of the human form in poses that we now identify as the posture of meditation.

The word philosophy means love of wisdom, and the study of philosophy provides a way in which human beings can investigate the nature of reality. Such a study naturally begins with personal pondering and leads to an exploration of the ideas of others. In ancient India, the sources of exposure to the ideas of others were the oral traditions, scriptures, and personal relationships with teachers. Once one had recognized the limitations of thought as a means for pursuing the heights of wisdom, one began true *sadhana* or spiritual practice, which, if performed with earnestness and devotion, could lead to the direct experience of reality.

Many of the early and subsequent writings from ancient India demonstrate that the heights and depths of reality had indeed been plumbed, and the truth of our existence had been realized and communicated. This knowledge has continued to be actively transmitted through the centuries. This great wisdom enters the world not only from the Hindu religion but from the roots of each of the world's great religions, several profound philosophies and our surviving shamanic traditions, all of which carry at their core the truth of our being.

The teachings contained in this book are universal, but they arose from the spiritual principles that gave rise to Hinduism. It is useful to note that the Hindu religion, while the most ancient of the great religions, is only the most recent form of a succession of religious and philosophical traditions dating back through the Bronze Age into prehistory. All of the other great religions of the world were founded during a roughly fixed period of time by a specific individual, dating back to Judaism's Abraham just prior to 2000 BCE. Hinduism is the only one of the world's great religions that arose from a primordial ancestry.

The oldest of the existing scriptures of the Indus region are the *Vedas* and the earliest of the *Upanishads* which, in written form, date back to 1500 BCE, but which are understood to have come into existence much earlier. Ethnologists speculate that these teachings were transmitted orally for centuries, and many in the contemporary Indian wisdom traditions insist that they were passed along in this fashion for millennia prior to a written form of their language.

By the 8th century of the current era, Buddhism was a major religious presence in India, and Hinduism was divided into many conflicting sects, each with its own set of beliefs and rituals. As happens with many religions over time, much of popular Hinduism had lost touch with its philosophical and spiritual roots. During this period, a man named Shankara absorbed and mastered the core teachings of the Hindu scriptures and reintroduced the basic principles of Hinduism to his contemporaries. He also clarified and emphasized the most fundamental aspect of truth by expounding a philosophy called *advaita* or nonduality.

Introduction

Shankara was a teacher of extraordinary accomplishment who had mastered the scriptures at an early age. He had a deep respect for the ancient wisdom that informed his native religion and he vowed to preserve it. Instead of rebelling against Hinduism or sowing the seeds of a new religion (witness Buddhism and Christianity), Shankara chose to remind his contemporaries of the deepest truths of their own scriptures. He wrote revelatory commentaries on many of the major Hindu texts including the *Upanishads*, the *Brahma Sutras*, and the *Bhagavad Gita*. All of these texts proclaim the numinous dimensions of human life and the fundamental truth of our existence.

Along with these commentaries, Shankara also wrote a few short treatises intended to simplify the often obscure teachings of the scriptures. The most widely known of these original works is the *Vivekachudamani*, or *The Crest Jewel of Discrimination*, which is available in many English translations. Another of these short works is the *Aparokshanubhuti*, known in English as *Self-Realization* or as *The Direct Experience* or *Intimate Cognition of Reality*. Here we find the essence of the teachings of Hinduism and discover not only the truths of the world's most ancient religion, but that same truth that is revealed in every great religious and spiritual tradition.

No English translation could presume to do justice to Shankara's original Sanskrit, but only a very few among us enjoy the ability to understand this ancient language, especially at the level required to appreciate the subtle and altogether radical concepts conveyed in such a text. This book is not another attempt at a word-for-word translation of these verses but, rather, a reverent paraphrase.

The 144 verses that follow have been composed from seven English language translations of the *Aparokshanubhuti*.[2] A comparison of the texts used to create this book displays abundant latitude in the translation and interpretation of each Sanskrit word or phrase, and yet, among them, there is an unmistakable allegiance to the spirit of the original work. In this translation, the wording of some of the verses has been expanded in the hope that a broader rendering, and occasional commentaries, might make the original ideas more accessible to the Western mind, and might ultimately lead the reader to the experience of Reality.

---

[2] See Appendix B.

The Experience of Reality

The Aparokshanubhuti
of Shankara

1. Here, at the very beginning, we offer profound homage, praise, and gratitude for the gift of this divine Knowledge which has the power to relieve us from ignorance.

Now, in this timeless moment, let us make a sincere gesture of reverence toward That which cannot be spoken or thought, That which is beyond all comprehension and yet without which nothing is; That to which we point in every direction, and which, for want of an adequate word, we call Reality, the first cause, the all-pervading essence, the Self of all, the highest happiness, the inmost desire of every heart.

2. The lessons set forth here can lead us to the realization of Knowledge beyond all imagining. These words have the power to reveal that which is not visible.

If we have been led to this precious instruction and are blessed with the desire to know the truth, then let us draw near and open our minds and hearts to this most perfect confidence. Let us return to it repeatedly and meditate upon the truth laid bare.

3. By the daily performance of the duties of our lives with earnestness and fidelity, and by the practice of selflessness and devotion, we can gain the qualities necessary for the realization of Truth.

4. The quality of detachment or dispassion means a gradual lessening of desire for the attractions of the world until all sense-objects, all the transitory and perishable "things" of life are viewed with calm indifference.

5. The Self is the Seer, the Witness, and does not come or go. The Self, the I Am, is eternally present and awake. Every other thing in existence, from a sunflower to the sun, appears and disappears on the screen of Awareness. To be able to distinguish the timeless from the temporal is known as discrimination.

6. The constant recognition and abandonment of desires and ambitions is called inner control. The recognition of the objects of sense as seductive, fleeting, and ultimately illusory is called outer control.

7. Turning away from the objects of sense is called detachment. Patiently bearing the pain and sorrow of life is known as endurance. These are conducive to happiness.

8. Trust in the teachings is called faith. A mind fixed firmly on ultimate Truth is called true concentration.

9. Oh my God, when and how shall I ever be free from the bondage of this ever-changing world? Thinking thus is called the desire for liberation.

10. One who has cultivated the qualities of discrimination, inner and outer control, patient endurance, concentration, and the desire for liberation; such a one, devoted to the highest good, is ready to turn to that Knowledge which is only available to the most perfect discernment.

11. Just as objects cannot be seen in the absence of light, so too, true Knowledge comes only with meditative inquiry.

12. Who am I? How did all of this come to be? Of what is the universe made? What is happening? Why am I here? This is the reasoning called inquiry.

13. I am not this body, which is only an aggregate of elements, nor am I this collection of senses; I am something different from these. This reasoning is called inquiry into truth.

14. The whole world is the product of ignorance and dissolves like a dream upon the dawn of true Knowledge. The real creator of the world is mental activity of many kinds. This is the reasoning resulting from inquiry into truth.

15. Just as a clay pot, no matter the size or shape, is made of earth and nothing else, so are the many, one. The dream is created by thought, and these two together are the product of Reality, of pure Being. The two arise from the One. This is the reasoning called inquiry into truth.

16. I am the One. I am the knower, the imperishable witness. I am the ever-existent and unchanging Self, beyond body and mind. I am the I Am. This is the reasoning that results from inquiry into truth.

17. This Self is my very Being, an undivided whole. This body is composed of many parts, ever-changing and short-lived. To imagine that the body could be this infinite Self is evidence of a great misunderstanding.

18. The Self is the inmost Spirit, the ruler of the body. The body is external in every respect and entirely subject to the laws of nature. To mistake the body for the Self is the greatest ignorance.

15

19. The Self is pure Consciousness and holy. The body is composed of flesh and fluids and subject to decay. How can the body be mistaken for the Self?

20. The Self is the illuminator of the universe and purity itself. The body is the source of confusion and ignorance. To mistake the body for the Self is to be lost in that ignorance.

21. The Self is pure Existence and timeless. The body is temporary and will soon cease to be. How can this body be mistaken for the Self?

22. Everything in the universe is illumined by the light of Consciousness, which is the Self. Physical light cannot compare to the effulgence of the Self, which shines even in darkness.

23. How strange that we temporarily inhabit this body and refer to it thus as, "my body," as if we possess it, the way we possess a pot or a cup, and yet we still imagine it to be who we are. This body is no different from any other object, and, like every object, it is limited, transitory, and not to be mistaken for the Self.

24. I am not this physical body, which lasts for only a moment. I am the one Reality, changeless and quiescent, the cause of Being and the source of consciousness and bliss. Knowledge of this is the highest wisdom.

25. Changeless am I, formless, immaculate, beyond space and time. How can I be this body which is never the same and subject to decay? This is called knowledge of the real.

26.　This Self is beyond imperfection, beyond illusion, beyond comprehension by the mind. The Self exists everywhere and pervades everything, whereas this body is doomed from the outset.

27.　This body is under the control of all the laws of nature, and finally unreal. I am beyond all qualities, unconditioned, perpetual and ever-free. How could this body contain me?

28.　The Self is without limits, imperishable, immovable, infinite and pure. The body is the very opposite of these qualities. How can I be that? This is called the knowledge of the wise.

29.　Only the ignorant think the body is real and the spirit is not real. Do not make this mistake. The Self is the only reality. Do not be fooled by appearances. The Self pervades the body but is independent of it. The body is entirely dependent and relative.

30.　Enough ignorance. We must come to know the Self. Study the scriptures and carefully and earnestly apply reasoning to this mystery. The Self is not a void. It is the source of our Existence and very difficult to see, hypnotized as we are by the body and the mind.

31.　The supreme Self is One and the same in each of us. It can be detected by the sense of "I," common to us all. Our bodies are many while the Self is One. Why do we confuse them?

32.   That which we call "I" is always the subject, while the body can only be an object of perception. When we refer to the body, we say, "This is my body." Why do we confuse the body with the Self?

33.   From infant to elder, there is never a moment when our bodies are not changing. As the body transforms from child to adult, our ideas and understanding also change. But the Self never changes. Our bodies and minds may be in constant flux, but our true identity is timeless and unchanging.

34.   Many are those wise ones who have discovered the secret of the Self through study of the scriptures. All the glories of the transcendental realms are inherent in this sublime Spirit, the one Self of all. How could this limited body contain the limitless Self?

35.   Again and again the scriptures declare that the whole of manifest existence is the Self and nothing else. How could this body contain the universe?

36.   The scriptures clearly state that the Self is beyond all conditions and limitations, pure and perfect. This body is bound at every turn by inescapable limitations; how could it be the conditionless Self?

37.   The Self shines by its own light, infinite and independent. The earthbound body is lit only from without. If not for the light of the Self, the body would be completely inert. How can we imagine that the body is who we are?

38. The most ancient scriptures, including those which prescribe rules for our behavior, declare that Spirit is different from the body and never ceases to exist, while the body will surely die, and soon. How can we confuse Spirit with the body?

39. Even the subtle energy body is composite and dependent. It is an ephemeral object of perception and therefore separate from the perceiver. Only the ignorant mistake the subtle body for the Self.

40. The Self is, in fact, the transcendental Lord of the universe and also the personal God. We feel the Self within the physical and subtle bodies as the indwelling Spirit. I am that Spirit. I am the Self of all. I am all, imperishable and beyond all.

41. To speak of the material body and to compare it to the Self might seem to lend some credibility to the body and to imply that the phenomenal world is real. But what purpose can be served by such thinking? The truth of our Being extends far beyond these fleeting appearances.

42. The body, gross and subtle, appears to exist only by the light of that supreme Reality known as the Self. Listen now to the reasoning that dissolves all differences.

43. Reality is Oneness beyond division. This Oneness is manifest as Awareness, and all that appears to exist has its being in Awareness. The conception of every thought, the perception of every phenomenon, each and all are appearances on the screen of Awareness. Just as a rope can appear to be a snake, so can the supreme Self appear to be a separate self. It is appearance only.

44. Absence of knowledge of the rope is the immediate cause of the appearance of the snake. Absence of knowledge of pure Awareness is the immediate cause of the appearance of the body and the world.

45. The One, the Absolute, is the sole cause of the material universe. There is no second thing. It follows, therefore, that this entire universe is nothing other than ultimate Reality.

46. The most holy of the scriptures declare that "All is One." All is this supreme Spirit, this pure Self, this ultimate Reality. There is no separate universe pervaded by the holy Spirit. The idea of the pervading and the pervaded is an illusion. There is only the One that is All. When we know this sacred Truth, how can we make distinctions? How can we see differences?

47. The great scriptures uniformly deny any multiplicity or distinction in the Oneness of the Absolute. How then can we imagine that the phenomenal universe is anything other than this same Absolute?

48. The scriptures decry the folly of seeing multiplicity in the part-less One. To see differences in the Undifferentiated is the height of calamity and necessarily leads to continued suffering.

49. All beings are born from this One which is supreme Spirit. All beings, therefore, are this ultimate Reality and nothing else. Be convinced of this.

50. The great scriptures insist that all apparent manifestations, all forms and the names that we assign to them, exist only within the underlying reality that is the Absolute. The many cannot exist except for the One.

51. The essential nature of a gold ring is gold alone. If a gold ring is refashioned into a pendant, the essential nature of the pendant is gold. Whatever the appearance, the gold is unaffected; so also with the changeless Spirit. No matter the form of manifestation, immutable Spirit is One.

52. If we forget that our essential nature is Spirit alone, if we think of ourselves as separate individuals, distinct from all other forms of creation, we are destined to feel the fear of extinction. If we know ourselves to be that One which is All, what is there to fear?

53. When we forget our oneness with all that is, we begin to perceive the duality of subject and objects, of self and others; but when we remember our true identity as the changeless Self of All, the illusion of separation vanishes. There is always only One.

54. When we realize that all apparently separate persons, places, and things are this One Self which we always are, we find ourselves free from delusion and misery; duality dissolves into nonduality.

55. The great scriptures declare that the true Self, our own infinite Being, is exactly that supreme Self, that ultimate Reality which is also the one Self of all and everything.

56. This world, though an object of our daily experience and serving practical purposes, is a dream-world. The dream we dream at night seems real until we wake, and our waking life seems real until we dream again. The world of our waking life is of the same order of experience as the dream world.

57.   When we are awake, the dream state does not exist. When we are dreaming, the waking state does not exist. Both dreaming and waking disappear in the deep sleep state, which, in turn, cannot exist in the waking or dreaming states.

58. Thus, all three states are not ultimately real. They, like all phenomena, are the result of the play of elements and qualities which, also, in the end, are without enduring reality. But the witness of all these states is timeless Being-Awareness. Everything that comes into existence is destined to pass away. Only the beginningless is endless.

59.   We might look at an exquisite piece of mother-of-pearl and imagine that it contains pure silver. After all, it appears to be even more perfectly silver than real silver. Sometimes we look at a beautiful pottery vase and imagine it to be something other than the clay from which it is made. Sometimes we look at ourselves and imagine that we are something other than supreme Spirit which is, in fact, all that we are.

60.   Just as a vase is only clay, the apparent silver is only mother-of-pearl, and a ring is nothing but gold, so is that which we call "myself" nothing other than the supreme Self of All, the One Reality. The appearance of an individual with a name and form and a separate existence is only a fleeting dream, soon to disappear.

61.   The blueness in the sky, the mirage in the desert, the form of a person superimposed upon a distant post, all illusions. So too is this universe taken to be separate from the One Self.

62   Just as a ghost may appear in empty space, or we might see an animal or a castle in the clouds; just as, when our eyes relax, we might see two moons in the sky, so does this universe appear before us. The universe appears because of the existence of Reality, which is also known as Consciousness and as the Self.

63.   A wave upon the ocean, no matter its shape or size, is made entirely of water. A copper vessel, no matter its shape or size, is made entirely of copper. This universe and every individual thing in this universe, no matter its shape or size, is made entirely of that nameless One that is the ground and cause of everything.

64.   Just as it is clay alone that appears as the many kinds of pottery, or thread alone that takes the name of cloth, so is it Consciousness alone that is referred to as the world. When we see beyond names and forms, we find the underlying Reality, the Truth that always is.

65.   Every single thing that happens in this world and in our lives, happens in and through this supreme Spirit, without which there would be nothing whatsoever. Millions of pieces of pottery fill our homes and marketplaces. They are not pots, jars, vases, bowls, cups, and mugs and pitchers, they are all made of one thing. They may appear to be different, but they are all the same.

66.   An earthen jar will never exist but for the clay from which it is made. Just so, this universe, and this self that we take ourselves to be, could not exist except for the existence of Reality which supports all appearances. Supreme Being is beyond cause; It gives rise to all the universes.

67. Every thought of the earthen jar includes an awareness of the earth through which it has its being. Sometimes the awareness is subtle, sometimes obvious and central to our appreciation of the vessel. It is the same with our awareness of the beginningless and ever-shining Spirit that underlies our every experience. We may not notice it, but it is always here; the only true and lasting part of the existence that we think of as "this life."

68. The rope is always a rope, it is never a snake. Though Awareness is pure and perfect, it appears to the ignorant as imperfect because we see only the world of objects and not the Self which is the cause of the world.

69. Just as the jar is nothing but earth, so is this body nothing but Consciousness, nothing but Spirit; so is this world only Awareness, only Spirit, the One Self. When we create such distinctions as "this is self" and "that is not self," we have missed the Oneness that is present in and as everything. Indeed, All is One.

70. To the hard-headed materialist, the body and the world are the only reality. When we see things in this way, the rope is always a snake and every mirage sends us scurrying after the illusion of water, or security, or happiness, none of which can be found in a mirage.

71. We see a beautiful clay pot and forget that it is nothing but earth. We hold a fine piece of clothing and forget that it is only thread. Unravel the thread and where is the cloth? So it is with that which we see in the mirror; remove the reality of the indwelling Spirit, our true and only identity, and where and of what use is the body, and who is there to see it?

72. We admire the glistening earring and forget that it is only gold. We watch the endless waves rolling in and forget that it is only water. We become hypnotized by the apparent drama in our lives and forget that all of it is Spirit dancing on the surface of the ocean of Existence.

73. A post in the distance is mistaken for a person. It is not a person, it is a post. A mirage appears to be water. It is not water, it is a mirage. The physical body, the face we see in the mirror, is thought to be our true identity. But the body is a dependent reality and not the final truth. Remember, there is only One.

74. A pile of timber may be assembled into a house, but the house is only wood. A heap of metal may be fashioned into a sword, but the sword is nothing but metal. The deathless Spirit takes on the appearance of a body and mind, but at no time is the apparent body-mind anything but pure Spirit.

75. We stand at the edge of the pond and see the nearby trees reflected on the surface of the water. We see the image of the tree, but it is only water. We look at ourselves and see and feel a body-mind, but it is only an image projected on the surface of Consciousness.

76. When we stand on the deck of a ship as it moves up river, we seem to be standing still and everything along the banks appears to be in motion. Similarly, we imagine that our bodies are moving through this busy world when in reality our true identity is stillness itself, ever-present Spirit, and life unfolds in this Being-Awareness, fully present right now.

77.   For a person suffering from jaundice, every white object appears to be yellow. When we do not understand the truth of the Self, every object we see appears to be real and we imagine that the body is who we are.

78.   To the nearsighted person, the world is blurry and indistinct. Just so, when we have not recognized the Self, we are not able to see things as they really are. We feel the presence of the Self and think that it is the body.

79.   We pull a firebrand from the flames and whirl it into the appearance of a fiery circle. But there is no circle of fire; there is only a point of light. We assume an identity upon our birth into this world and soon find our lives whirling through a circle of events. But it only appears to be a circle of events; all phenomena are nothing but timeless Awareness, the source of this universe and this moment.

80.   Just as a grand and inspiring object, when seen at a distance, appears to be small and insignificant, so too, without true Knowledge, does the infinite Self appear to be as small and insignificant as the physical body.

81.   We are only able to acknowledge the existence of tiny waterborne creatures after they have been made visible to us with the use of a lens. So too, without direct experience, we are reluctant to concede the existence of an ultimate Consciousness and thus we continue to insist that the body is who we are.

82. In the distance, we glimpse a pane of glass lying in the road and mistake it for a puddle of water. Looking more closely, we can see the truth. When we are born into the pains and pleasures associated with this body, we naturally take it to be the only reality. On closer inspection, often prompted by the words of the wise, we may see beyond our first impressions and recognize the Reality behind the appearance.

83. If we were to happen upon a glowing ember on the path, it might appear to us as a lost ruby. Similarly, if we were to see a lost ruby lying on the pathway, we might mistake it for a glowing ember. In either case, closer inspection would reveal the truth. If we were to inspect ourselves more closely, we would discover that this body is merely an object of awareness, while the Self *is* that Awareness.

84. When the clouds are moving swiftly, the moon seems to be running through the sky, and yet we know that the moon does not move so rapidly. We can tell the difference between appearance and reality. Yet when the body is busy and the mind is full, we are unable to recognize the stillness of the Self that is always present, supporting our every thought and deed.

85. We are hiking through the woods. We decide to leave the trail and take a shortcut. A few minutes later, we slip in the leaves and fall to the ground. When we finally get to our feet, we realize that, without the path to guide us, we have become disoriented. It may take a few moments before we are able to get our bearings. It could take much longer. If we continue to insist that this body is who we are, we could be lost for a lifetime.

86. Reflected in still water, the image of the moon is still. When the wind disturbs the surface of the water, the image of the moon becomes distorted. When the clear light of Consciousness is reflected in an agitated mind, the world takes on a confusing appearance; the unreal is mistaken for reality. Just as the moon is untouched by the changeful nature of wind and water, so Awareness is always shining, unaffected by the movements of the mind.

87. The body and the world appear to be real until the Self is directly experienced. Once the Self, the Truth of Awareness, has come to light, the conviction "I am the body" naturally dissolves.

88. When the whole of the universe, animate and inanimate, is known to depend for its existence upon the Self, the Reality of Awareness, where is the justification for imagining the physical body to be the Self?

89. Oh, You Intelligent One, who are drawn to these words; attend to them. Give yourself to contemplation of this supreme Wisdom which is the highest good of all beings and the ultimate purpose of every life. The vagaries of destiny are of no importance for one who lives in the knowledge of the One Spirit also known as the Self.

90. Many scriptures contend that one remains subject to the consequences of one's past actions until the debt has been paid, even though one should be otherwise liberated through direct knowledge of the Self. This view is hereby refuted.

91. When the sleeper awakes, the dream disappears. When we detect and recognize the self-luminous light of Awareness, we immediately understand the relativity and impermanence of the world of appearances. The body is known to be an illusion and destiny is rendered meaningless. We are the One Self of All and this mental organism is a dream from which we are soon to awaken.

92. Many are they who point to the effects of past actions and insist upon the reality of reincarnation. But for those who have realized their identity as the unborn and deathless Spirit, such notions are no more real than last night's dream.

93. Just as the dream body is superimposed upon the mind, so is the physical body appearance only and ultimately unreal. How can such a temporary thing as this body be thought to be born into eternal life? The timeless Self exists before and after the body.

94. The greatest scriptures declare the unreality of the phenomenal world and point to the indescribable Absolute as the ultimate Truth. The world as we know it exists only in the absence of this supreme Knowledge.

95. The rope in our path is always and forever a rope. It can never be a snake, no matter how deluded and convinced we may become. The world that we live in, that appears to us to be so real, is always and forever changeless Spirit alone.

96. When we realize that the snake in our path is only a rope, the illusion disappears in an instant, just so, when the Absolute is recognized, all separate things dissolve into the nameless One.

97.   When it is finally acknowledged that the world and the universe which contains it are not ultimately real, it follows that the body, which is contained in the world, is also not real. It is only for those who identify with their bodies and their thoughts that teachings are provided regarding destiny and the fruits of action.

98.   When one realizes the nondual Truth of Existence, one is immediately freed from the web of the world. The life of the individual soul becomes an appearance only, no more real than any other dream.

99.   If, however, even after careful reasoning, we still cling to the idea of a separate self, we risk becoming embroiled in the absurdity of disagreeing with the holy teachings and thereby diminishing the possibility of being liberated in this lifetime. For if we refuse to embrace the nondual conclusion of divine Truth, we are condemned to a merely relative existence, bound irrevocably by the pairs of opposites.

100.   Now are to be expounded the fifteen steps necessary for the attainment of direct knowledge of Reality. With the help of these guides, one should practice profound meditation upon the Holy Truth at all times.

101.   Without constant and steady practice, one cannot hope to realize that Reality which is the source of the life force and is, in fact, Awareness Itself. Therefore one must be earnest and persistent in the practice of meditation upon this Infinite Truth.

102-103. The following fifteen steps can lead to the Direct Experience of Reality. The steps are: control of the senses, control of the mind, renunciation, silence, space, time, posture, control of the nervous system, equilibrium, firmness of vision, control of the vital forces, withdrawal of the mind from the objects of sense, concentration, contemplation of the Self, and absorption. We will now examine these steps in order and consider the deeper meaning of each.

104. The restraint of the senses is not the product of refusing to see and hear and think and feel, but rather to constantly hold the conviction that "all of this is God."

105. To cultivate and perpetuate a unitive thought such as "Only Consciousness is real" or "All is One," to the exclusion of all other kinds of thought, is known as control of the mind. The recognition of the light of Awareness as one's true Identity brings the very highest happiness. This the wise practice with diligence.

106. True renunciation does not consist in turning one's back on the things of the world, but in seeing every object of perception as Awareness alone. When Reality dawns, illusions disappear, attachments fall away without aversion or effort, and things are seen as they are.

107. Even when speaking, the wise should always strive to be one with that Great Silence from which words, together with the mind, turn back, baffled by its perfection. This is the practice of silence.

The Experience of Reality

108. Who can describe That Supreme Spirit from which words turn away? Even the phenomenal world is beyond description, how much more so the Realm of the Absolute? When nothing can be said, what is there to say?

109. That state of being which is beyond expression gives birth to true silence which naturally arises when there are no adequate words. The mere restraint of speech is prescribed only for those who cannot approach stillness in the real way.

110. By the practice of place is meant abidance in the solitude of pure space, where neither thought nor the universe ever began or existed. From this place where nothing is, all things appear. The universe is born of this Reality.

111. Timeless Reality is prior to all existence; it is manifest as Awareness of the universe as it appears in the blink of an eye and disappears in another blink. This is known as the practice of time.

112. The proper posture is that inner state which permits the uninterrupted contemplation of our true being. This is the real posture and not those physical postures that merely disturb our ease and happiness.

113. The lauded first cause of all beings, the timeless support of the universe, in which enlightened beings are merged and immersed, this Being-Awareness is the real position, the true posture.

114.   This nameless Reality, the root of all existence, is the only worthy object of meditation, the only sure means of restraining the mind. To bind the heart and mind to this ultimate and inconceivable One is to be rooted in the Ground of Being.

115.   When the mind is fully absorbed in contemplation of this infinite Being that we are, the body and mind naturally fall into equilibrium. The mere straightening of the limbs is of little use.

116.   One should learn to direct one's vision by recalling that the image of the world is Consciousness only and not what appears to the eye. This is called noble vision.

117.   Or, let the vision be turned towards That in which the separation of the seer, the seeing, and the seen dissolves into unity. What good is staring at the tip of one's nose?

118.   Learn to quiet all the disturbances in the mind by recognizing them as nothing but ripples in the ocean of Consciousness. All mental objects are Consciousness alone. Living in this Awareness is true control of the vital forces.

119.   True breath control is to see all as One. For those who insist upon breathing practices, let them discover the real breath. The real in-breath consists of holding the continuous thought, "I am this witnessing Awareness." The recognition of the unreality of all phenomena, including the body, the mind, and the universe is the aspect of breathing known as the real breathing out.

120. Let the restraint of the breath be an opportunity to stabilize in the true Self as the source and totality of Being. This is the true method of breathing for the wise and not those popular breathing exercises that only torture the nose.

121. When everything that appears in the mind and senses is known to be the Self, we are practicing the true withdrawal of the senses. When the mind is merged in infinite Consciousness, all objects of perception disappear and the resplendent Self is revealed. This is the practice of the wise.

122. No matter how active the mind becomes, no matter where it wanders, true concentration is to recognize that Consciousness alone is the underlying reality, and all thoughts and all experiences, be they grave or glorious, are transient and relative. Realizing the truth of the Self, we hold steady in the knowledge that Awareness alone is real.

123. We become independent of the movements of the mind through cultivating the unassailable thought, "I am none other than this pure witnessing Awareness." This is called meditation.

124. Letting thought subside while holding onto the feeling that "There is only this Being/Awareness" leads to the dissolution of thought. We dissolve into changelessness and silence. This is known as absorption. It is also called real Knowledge.

125. This best of practices should be undertaken regularly until, having become a natural part of one's life, it arises spontaneously and is always close at hand.

126.   Once the Self is realized, the need for steps and practices falls away. We are what we are. Such a condition cannot be imagined. Who can describe Being?

127.   The practice of silence and self-knowledge is likely to be hampered by obstacles. Among the most common difficulties are idleness, boredom, pointless thoughts not devoted to the holy ideal, and the desire for sensory enjoyment.

128.   Other obstacles to absorption in the Self are lack of concentration, distraction by pleasures and pains, paralysis of the intellect, fatigue and sleep, to name a few. Each of these distractions must be met as it arises. The fruitfulness of our practice depends upon how we relate to these diversions.

129.   When the mind focuses upon an object, that object fills the mind. By thinking of the void, the mind becomes objectless and empty. When the mind is fixed upon The Absolute, the mind will be filled with the glory of the transcendental Spirit that manifests as all the universes. Therefore, we should constantly think of that One which is beyond thought until there is only One.

130.   Those of us who do not center our lives around the holy truth surely live in vain. Though we may exist like other living beings, if we are oblivious to our reason for being, we have squandered this precious incarnation.

131.   Blessed are those wise ones who heed the call of Truth and taste Reality. They are worthy of praise and are sure to grow in completeness and joy.

132.   There are some among us who have embraced this Knowledge so completely that they have been absorbed into the supreme Spirit even while they live. They are not to be confused with those who merely talk about the supreme state but do not strive to attain it.

133.   Many of us are skillful in speaking about the Holy Spirit but we have no direct experience to enliven our message. We have not undertaken true spiritual practice and we remain entangled in the affairs of the world. We inflict our ignorance upon others and actively perpetuate our own separation from the very God we profess to represent

134.   The true aspirant does not allow a single mental moment to pass that does not hold the Absolute as both the background and centerpiece of every experience. Each moment arises within this holy framework.

135.   The cause may be reflected in the effect, but the effect can never illuminate the real cause. The entire universe is merely an effect and eventually is recognized as unreal. When the mind is brought to stillness by deep contemplation, all phenomena cease to exist. The effect disappears and, with it, the imagined cause. In this way we realize That which is Absolute, nondual, beyond the causal principle, beyond the realm of things, pure Existence, pure Intelligence; Bliss.

136.   Thus we find ourselves in that state in which all distinction and separation has dissolved into the causeless and relationless One. Here we find no place for words or thought. Remember the illustration of the earth that makes up every sort of pottery. So does everything that appears to be, exist in name only. In Truth, there is only the nameless Absolute.

137. Practicing in this way, cultivating stillness and discriminating between the real and the impermanent, there dawns in the mind the recognition of our identity as the infinite Self. Then we know the pure-minded state of awareness and enjoy supreme happiness.

138. We can develop greater clarity by seeing all things in the universe as the effects of a single cause, the Absolute, the One. Then we discern the existence of this One Self everywhere, inherent in every phenomenon, in each living being and every drop of water.

139. Thus is the cause seen in every effect. As the mind returns to stillness, the individual effects dissolve into that stillness. As the effects disappear, so does the cause cease to have meaning. In this way we transcend the causal relationship and remain as That which is nondual and prior to everything: Being, Consciousness, Bliss.

140. Our true nature is divine. It is only our inability to accept our inherent divinity that perpetuates the illusion of a separate individual. If we allow ourselves to embrace the holy teachings as T ruth and meditate upon this Oneness, we find ourselves to be the Truth. If we were to cultivate the unshakable conviction that we truly are the divine Being described in the holy scriptures, we would realize this Reality which we already are.

141. This whole world, visible and invisible, is born entirely of Consciousness. By virtue of our own experience, our own undeniable Existence, our meditation will lead us to confess, "I am this Awareness."

142. We should look upon every object of perception as a simple manifestation of Consciousness. Thereby we come to know that each and every thing that appears before us is Consciousness alone. Thus are we freed from the tyranny of appearances, and thus do we come to live in the freedom and felicity of the natural state, resting in the bliss of pure Awareness, the true Self.

143. These fifteen steps of spiritual practice herein described comprise the true royal path to realization of absolute Truth and the freedom that attends it. These steps are not to be confused with those lesser practices which occupy the energies of most aspirants. These steps may be combined with more physical routines for those who are only partially prepared for the demands of committed spiritual practice.

144. Those whose minds and hearts are ripe for this great Knowledge, and who are earnest and devoted to the highest good, will find this a most accessible and productive method for realizing the ultimate Truth of this life.

The Experience of Reality

The Aparokshanubhuti
of Shankara

with commentary

1. Here, at the very beginning, we offer profound homage, praise, and gratitude for the gift of this divine Knowledge which has the power to relieve us from ignorance.

Now, in this timeless moment, let us make a sincere gesture of reverence toward That which cannot be spoken or thought, That which is beyond all comprehension and yet without which nothing is; That to which we point in every direction, and which, for want of an adequate word, we call Reality, the first cause, the all-pervading essence, the Self of all, the highest happiness, the inmost desire of every heart.

2. The lessons set forth here can lead us to the realization of Knowledge beyond all imagining. These words have the power to reveal that which is not visible.

If we have been led to this precious instruction and are blessed with the desire to know the truth, then let us draw near and open our minds and hearts to this most perfect confidence. Let us return to it repeatedly and meditate upon the truth laid bare.

3. By the daily performance of the duties of our lives with earnestness and fidelity, and by the practice of selflessness and devotion, we can gain the qualities necessary for the realization of Truth.

3. The qualities referred to in this verse are traditional requisites for spiritual development, past and present. Shankara will address many of these in the coming verses. The first of these qualities is discernment or discrimination between the real and the unreal, between the timeless and the transient, between what is finally true and what is only apparent or relative.

41

The Experience of Reality

Another quality is dispassion or detachment from the many objects of perception that join to make up our world. As spiritual understanding grows, the transitory experiences of life cease to satisfy our growing taste for the limitless.

The regulation of thought is also a necessary part of spiritual development and eventually gives rise to the recognition of our identity as the witness of the stream of thoughts. This discovery represents a milestone in spiritual life and marks the start of the process of disidentification from the thinking mind.

Other important qualities are the ability to concentrate one's mind, calmness, control of the senses, patience, tolerance, and the ability to withdraw from the dissonance of both the external and internal worlds and return to the stillness within. An especially important quality for the realization of Truth is unshakable faith that the Truth can be known.

Perhaps the most indispensable quality of all is the earnest desire for liberation that appears in our lives as we realize how completely we are caught in the web of concepts, lost in the dream of a physical universe and an individual human life that is separate from everything else.

Once we realize that we are lost in a collective illusion, and once this holy longing for reality has taken root, the other spiritual qualities gradually reveal themselves as having been present all along, lying dormant until we recognize the dream that we had taken to be our real life. Once we awaken *to* the dream, we also begin to awaken *from* the dream.

4. The quality of detachment or dispassion means a gradual lessening of desire for the attractions of the world until all sense-objects, all the transitory and perishable "things" of life are viewed with calm indifference.

4. One of the foundations of spiritual life, and an inevitable product of spiritual practice, is a sense of detachment from the attractions of the world and a growing inclination to disengage ourselves from *all* mental objects in order to allow our natural inner stillness to reveal itself and make the mind available for contemplation.

When the mind is attracted to some objects and repelled by others, our attention is overpowered by extraneous thoughts and feelings. We may find ourselves "hooked" by things we like and also by things we dislike.

Detachment does not imply a sense of aversion toward the objects of the senses and the world, but a simple recognition of the limited value of the things which, at an earlier time, may have seemed important. Wealth, status, comfort, pleasure, and the attempt to fulfill recurrent desires are all gradually replaced by the subtle but much more fulfilling qualities of contentment, equanimity, and peaceful joy.

5. The Self is the Seer, the Witness, and does not come or go. The Self, the I Am, is eternally present and awake. Every other thing in existence, from a sunflower to the sun, appears and disappears on the screen of Awareness. To be able to distinguish the timeless from the temporal is known as discrimination.

5. Things that are seen and touched and felt and thought have a beginning and an end; they are transient, provisional, and dependent for their reality. It makes no difference if these things are sacred or mundane. To the degree that they appear in consciousness, they are separate, they are objects of perception, things that are seen. Only seeing is finally true.

The Being-Awareness that is our true Self is independent of all externals. Even God is a concept. This does not mean that God is non-existent; it means that any and all *concepts* of God are necessarily limited, incomplete, not true. Shankara would contend that the word "God," in its popular context, is a product of dualistic thinking and is equivalent to the Hindu deities of his own era, Brahma, the creator, Vishnu, the preserver, and Shiva, the destroyer, as well as Ishvara, the personal deity and collective God, all of which are also merely concepts. In this view, God is an imaginary term juxtaposed with the material world and furnished with those qualities ascribed to the Hindu trinity as well as the inclusive characteristics of Ishvara, the Supreme Lord. This God creates and determines the world and can be responsive to petition. For Shankara, this God is a fantasy, created by the minds that conceive it, and no more real than the illusory world it populates. But it is necessarily from this world of illusion that we begin our investigation of Reality, and "God" is the highest form of the illusion, the closest that concepts can bring us to this most transcendental Truth.

For this reason, and to minimize confusion, the word God is used sparingly. There are several adequate synonyms that carry less residual meaning and do not prompt our minds to project our ingrained definitions into this conversation. That which is represented by the word God is Reality Itself, that nameless, formless One which is all, and before all, and beyond all.

Verse 5 states, "The Self, the I am, is eternally present and awake." Few of us would claim that this statement is true of ourselves. We may be physically present all the time, but we are certainly not awake all the time, and our presence is occasionally in body only, since, even when awake, our minds are often lost in thought, far away from our immediate physical circumstances. So the Self to which Shankara refers is clearly not the self that we have spent our lives cultivating and protecting.

Verse 5 implies that the Self is who we *really* are, beyond our thoughts and feelings about our identity. The use of the term "Self" is often a cause of confusion. Like the word "God", we have assigned specific meanings to "self" which have little correspondence to transcendental Reality.

Especially in the West, it is difficult for us to reconcile these concepts, so it is our good fortune that Shankara intends to relieve us of our puzzlement by guiding us to the direct experience of the Self. We have already had ample experience of this separate self that we have taken ourselves to be, so the contrast between the two should make it easy for us to distinguish one from the other. At the risk of spoiling the ending, it should be obvious that, however divided and schizophrenic we may feel from time to time, there are *not* two selves whereby one can know the other. Whatever we may experience that "feels real" to us cannot be the whole truth, because only the Knower is real. When Reality dawns, even the knowing disappears into That which is.

The perfection that is the Self cannot be claimed by the apparent individual because each of us, as separate entities, is a temporary manifestation. Our bodies are composed of many forms of energy, most notably matter, and all of these forms are ultimately unreal; they come into being, exist for a while in the manifest universe and then dissolve back into their elements. No exceptions.

Every single thing is a temporary thing, "from Brahman to a blade of grass," all equally ephemeral. But how could God, or the Hindu term, Brahman, the immanent and transcendent divine ground of all and everything, be impermanent? Simply because Brahman, like the Western word God, is only a thought, an object of conception, and therefore unreal. What Brahman really is, what God really is, is the Absolute, the Seer of all that is seen, the Self, the formless, changeless, timeless, pure and perfect, ultimate Reality. And this nondual One does not leave room for the appearance of any other thing, including an individual that could know this truth as separate from itself. So we find ourselves face to face with the great mystery of the One: If there is only this One and yet we are here, how could we not *be* this one?

This great mystery is called Brahman or God or the Self; It is That which alone is. This great mystery is the ultimate Truth which illuminates each object as it arises. What objects arise? Anything, everything, but most especially *us*. We arise *as* and are illuminated *by* the light of the Self. Our bodies, our minds and our feelings are all ultimately temporary and thus unreal, and yet we experience this existence because the Absolute *is* real.

With our mind and our emotions we interpret and respond to the sensory impressions that make up our life experiences and give them definition and meaning, some held roughly in common, but all necessarily our own. Each of us creates the world in which we live, and all of it, from the formless God to each blade of grass, is ultimately unreal. So what is real? We are. This Being that we feel, this formless Presence in the world of form, this changeless Witness of perpetual change; this is what we are. This idea held with conviction is called discrimination of the real.

The Experience of Reality

6. The constant recognition and abandonment of desires and ambitions is called inner control. The recognition of the objects of sense as seductive, fleeting, and ultimately illusory is called outer control.

6. A spiritual life is usually a peaceful life. This does not mean that spiritual people withdraw to caves or monasteries or close themselves up in their homes. It means that, in the midst of what are often very busy lives, such people enjoy an inner quiet. They may be talking constantly, listening carefully or engaging in complex physical or mental activities, and yet be firmly rooted in deep knowing which exists wholly within and yet entirely beyond the events of the moment.

This is not to suggest that such people always appear peaceful or behave calmly; they may or they may not, but underneath their outer appearance and behavior lies a deep peace which permeates and transcends the visible circumstances of their lives.

How do we find this sort of peace for ourselves? Some teachers insist that happiness and peace are always present and active deep within us, but we do not know it, we cannot feel it. If we are peaceful and happy, we are relaxed, we are content, and we are engaged in the present moment. If we find that we are not happy, if our peace is disturbed, it is because we want things to be different than the way they are. In short, we want, and in our wanting we forget what we have, what we are.

The light of Spirit shines like the sun, but unlike our sun, the light of Spirit never began and will never end. If we are open and receptive, free from preoccupation and conflict, the light of Spirit shines in us like the sun shining in a cloudless sky. But what if we *are* preoccupied? What if we are frequently thinking about our bodies or our reputations, our health or our bank accounts, our plans for the future or the endless problems in our lives and the lives of our family and our world? These are the clouds that obscure that clear light of the Spirit that is always shining just beyond the clouds.

Aparokshanubhuti with commentary

It is only natural that we consider problematic issues from time to time, but much of our mental activity seems to be out of our control. Wants and worries can occupy our thoughts and cloud our minds so thoroughly that the ever-present light of Spirit is obscured and our peaceful center seems miles away.

In this verse, Shankara points out the spiritual principles and practices that can free us from these limitations, these clouds that obscure our higher vision and separate us from the freedom and fullness that lie just behind our thoughts and feelings.

One of the most helpful of these practices is to notice our thoughts and feelings immediately upon their appearance. Once we have become attuned to the subtle agitation that arises when we experience the desire for things to be different than they are, we can judge whether an issue is important and needs to be considered and acted upon, or whether it has just arisen in our thoughts because of our personal tendencies and mental habits. This is known as inner control; the ability to recognize objects as they arise in consciousness, and to choose whether to entertain these thoughts and feelings, or to allow them to recede back into infinite silence.

Another quality of growth into the fulfillment of spiritual life is known as outer control. This is the ability to choose which of the myriad sense impressions that make up our environment will be allowed into our direct experience. We naturally find ourselves attracted by those sensory objects to which our individual tendencies are inclined. Every time we find ourselves captivated by something, we have an opportunity to weigh the importance of attending to the alluring sensation at the potential expense of our inherent tranquility, the peaceful joy which, left undisturbed, is our natural state.

This is the meaning of outer control: to be able to say yes or no to the objects and opportunities that life places before us. It may seem easy enough to simply choose what we want and consequently what we think about, but the tendencies that have taken root in us have a powerful influence. Before we know it, we are consumed by thoughts and emotions. These thoughts, and the associations and actions they generate, can be so seductive that it may be hours, days, or most of a lifetime before we realize

47

that we have lost touch with our inherent peacefulness, our true nature.

We can avoid these lapses by bringing our attention to the contents of consciousness, to the totality of our lives, so that when attractions and desires arise, we have the opportunity to make a choice. If the attraction feels too strong to allow us the freedom to choose, we can at least be fully aware of how, once again, we have been overcome by the wiles of the world. This provides an additional opportunity to practice inner control as we exercise our freedom to decline the further indulgences of judgment and self-condemnation.

Shankara tells us that there is another approach to spiritual fulfillment; a more direct approach that sees beyond the need for inner and outer control. His great gift to us is to repeatedly bring us back to the One, to the unified whole that is both the source and the goal of life.

Throughout these 144 verses we will be reminded that there is only One, and that all phenomena are simply manifestations of this nameless ground of Being. Shankara encourages us to look beyond all appearances and attend instead to That from which everything arises. "That" is This; this Awareness that *is* this very moment, this word, this Being that we are right now. To feel this being directly is to experience Reality. By means of this singular practice we can arrive at true freedom and unassailable peace; to knowledge beyond words and joy beyond description.

7. Turning away from the objects of sense is called detachment. Patiently bearing the pain and sorrow of life is known as endurance. These are conducive to happiness.

7. As the light of spiritual awareness dawns in our lives, we find ourselves naturally less attracted to our usual preferences and habitual patterns of gratification. We discover that we do not have to force ourselves to give up the things we thought we wanted, because many of our most persistent attachments simply fall away, and all the while, as naturally as any flower, we draw ever closer to the light.

This does not mean that the conflict and pain that are a natural part of life will suddenly disappear. Life in its fullness still continues, with all of its intrinsic pleasure and pain, loss and gain. But with the realization of our true nature, we find ourselves patiently and peacefully bearing the sorrow and suffering of life. It is called patient endurance; it is called joyful forbearance; it is called love.

As love rises up from within, we are gradually relieved of our normal tendency to make distinctions and entertain preferences. Everything shares the same beauty, everything is the same size. From the world's most perfectly cut diamond to a pebble on the path, there is no difference. Everything gleams with its own perfection.

8. Trust in the teachings is called faith. A mind fixed firmly on ultimate Truth is called true concentration.

8. There is good reason to relate to the great scriptures of the world as beneficent and authoritative instruction. These spiritual teachings have our best interests at heart and we will benefit from allowing ourselves to trust them. These teachings have been handed down through the ages to bring us peace and inner freedom in the midst of our otherwise ordinary lives.

The great scriptures were written to speak to many levels of understanding. Certain of these writings contain instructions that reveal the basic truths of our lives and provide us with methods whereby we can experience these truths for ourselves. These teachings arise from depths of knowledge and wisdom and from heights of transcendental consciousness that have been reached by relatively few. The people who communicate these ideas to us do so because they have known the unspeakable joy of direct knowledge and the all-encompassing love that arises with it. Their greatest wish is that each of us would discover this peace and joy. There is no greater gift to give or receive.

The cultivation of concentration is a hallmark of many spiritual disciplines. The ability to fix the mind upon a chosen object is considered indispensable for success in traditional spiritual practice. If we have some experience with meditation, we can appreciate how difficult it is to keep the mind focused on a single point. In fact, most of our popular meditation techniques are specifically designed to strengthen concentration. The goal of focused attention is freedom from extraneous mental activity which obscures our vision and dilutes our powers of perception.

Shankara, however, is not only concerned with the activities we adopt as means for undertaking spiritual practice. He is determined that we come to understand the big picture. He implies that struggling to reach some distant point where we will achieve our spiritual birthright only strengthens the illusion that we are an unfinished individual who must work diligently to destroy our encumbrances.

In response to this misunderstanding, Shankara continues his no-nonsense approach to our spiritual search by circumventing the whole issue of concentration as a potential stumbling block to our success and a necessary part of our preparation. He wants us to understand that concentration is like a light which we shine on any object that we want to see more clearly. The brighter the light, the more clarity we experience. But the crucial issue is not the strength of the light, but rather, where we choose to point it.

Developing the ability to concentrate does not require that we undertake a rigorous program of mental exercises, like focusing on a single mental object or attending to sense perceptions for prolonged periods without distraction. The kind of concentration that serves us best comes from being interested, from being fully engrossed in each moment. Concentration comes from *caring* about what is happening in this moment. Shankara encourages us to remember what we are doing and why. There is an absolute Reality underlying this dreamlike life that we are living. We may not know what it is, but we can know *that* it is. Once we have discovered that it is possible to be truly awake, how can we be content to remain asleep? When we see confusion and suffering arising in our lives, and in the lives of those around us, we may even begin to feel that we have an obligation to awaken to this nameless and ultimate Truth. As this "awakening" dawns in us, true concentration is born. Now it has a new name; it is called love.

9. Oh my God, when and how shall I ever be free from the bondage of this ever-changing world? Thinking thus is called the desire for liberation.

9. There is a popular expression in some communities of spiritual seekers known as "wanting to want God." This suggests that we understand that we must have our priorities straight if we intend to pursue a spiritual path, but there are so many attractions and distractions in our lives that we feel ourselves to be side-tracked, off course, and unable to fully commit to what "God" requires. We imagine that, if we truly want God, we will do whatever it takes to find God; and if we are perpetually distracted by our mental and emotional lives, then we clearly do not "want" God enough and can only wish that we did.

Verse 9 speaks of the "bondage of this ever-changing world." This bondage is created by the illusion that there is a vast distance between us and God. Shankara, in his compassion for our imagined predicament, is giving us the means to recognize the truth of our existence and to identify the apparent obstacles that separate us from our true being.

Everyone knows the feeling of being unable to control what is going on in the mind. There are a host of states of mind that keep us firmly enmeshed in this ever-changing world. Among these are worry, infatuation, desire, jealousy, aversion, envy, distrust, anger, agitation, depression, malaise, impatience, restlessness, laziness, and fear. Once we appreciate how severely we are hobbled by these mental and emotional encumbrances, the desire for real freedom naturally arises. Only then will we begin in earnest.

10. One who has cultivated the qualities of discrimination, inner and outer control, patient endurance, concentration, and the desire for liberation; such a one, devoted to the highest good, is ready to turn to that Knowledge which is only available to the most perfect discernment.

10. The knowledge spoken of here is of a different order than ordinary knowledge, consisting of facts and information. This is

The Experience of Reality

a knowledge that no amount of thinking can reveal, but which arises spontaneously within us when the mind runs out of thoughts and is extinguished like a fire with no more fuel to burn. The qualities outlined in verse 10 make us ready for such revelation, in part by gradually suffusing us with mental quiet, revealing the spaciousness that is within us, the silent Beingness that is our essence and very Self.

When the Oracle utters the words, "Know Thyself," this is the knowledge that is commended to us. This Self-knowledge relieves us of everything extraneous, including our personal identity. There is no longer an entity who can claim knowledge of any sort. There is only what is.

Of this knowledge it has been said that, if we have it, we do not need anything else, and if we do not have it, it doesn't matter much what else we have.

11. Just as objects cannot be seen in the absence of light, so too, true Knowledge comes only with meditative inquiry.

11. Meditative inquiry is recommended to us because thought cannot contain this knowledge. Most of us are plunged into confusion when trying to consider a type of knowledge that is beyond thought. Where else, besides thought, could knowledge possibly be? Happily, the solution to such a quandary lies in a lighthearted response to the problem: don't think about it.

In meditative inquiry we make an art and a science of the strategy called "don't think about it." If we trust the teachings, as Shankara suggests in verse 8, and thus take it on faith that this knowledge is beyond the scope of thought, then we can relax our natural need to understand, to make sense of this information that is appearing before us. Then, meditative inquiry will be a simple process of abiding in stillness, not seeking knowledge or experience of any kind, but simply allowing ourselves to rest in the Beingness that, deep down, we always are. Knowledge arises in us directly, not mediated by thoughts which normally label and categorize our every experience. The knowledge that comes from direct experience is pre-conceptual, intuitive, and innate. Meditative inquiry affords us a way to be in relationship to these

teachings with nothing more than a simple desire to learn, and a
willingness to look where the teachings are pointing.

Answers seldom come without questions and knowledge of
Reality rarely arises without inquiry. Meditative inquiry compels
us to rest in stillness, for the question we ask is too big for words
or thoughts. We simply shine the light of our attention into
unfathomable emptiness and rest in our own Being-Awareness.
True Knowledge *is* this Being-Awareness.

*12. Who am I? How did all of this come to be? Of what is the
universe made? What is happening? Why am I here? This is the
reasoning called inquiry.*

12. Many of us ask these questions early on in our lives.
Shankara encourages us to ask questions right now. Let us ask
the big questions: What is real? What is finally true?

Some of us are comfortable without asking such questions,
while others are content to accept the answers supplied by our
culture of origin. Some insist upon exploring such questions on
our own. We examine every answer we discover, earnestly
seeking and searching in many directions. We will be satisfied
only when we have realized the answers from within ourselves.

Without this kind of inquiry, the illusions of the world and
the discrete individual remain intact. Once inquiry begins, even
the inquirer is carefully examined and every cherished truth is
called into question. The eventual fruit of inquiry is peace and
freedom from ignorance.

*13. I am not this body, which is only an aggregate of
elements, nor am I this collection of senses; I am something
different from these. This reasoning is called inquiry into truth.*

13. Here we address the first question posed in the previous
verse: Who am I? Here also is our first exposure to a teaching
that will be repeated many times in this book. When the
knowledge being transmitted is as simple as "I am not this
body," we may have to hear it more than once if it is to penetrate

to our intuition which, unlike the intellect, is equipped to comprehend such a notion. Thus far, Shankara has only hinted at who or what we are, but he clearly starts us upon the path of inquiry by telling us what we are not.

Our initial inquiry may need to be based upon a degree of faith in the scriptures or in the teachings of those we have reason to trust. We may be so skeptical about the radical declarations that Shankara puts forth that the best we can muster is a willingness to hear him out. After all, there is little immediate evidence to support the contention that we are not the body. If we happen to drop a can of soup on our foot, the body certainly feels real enough. There is no evidence that we existed before the body came into being, and we cease to live and function when the body dies, so how are we to see ourselves as something other than this body? This is the meaning of inquiry.

14. The whole world is the product of ignorance and dissolves like a dream upon the dawn of true Knowledge. The real creator of the world is mental activity of many kinds. This is the reasoning resulting from inquiry into truth.

14. The second question in verse 12 is answered here: How did all of this come to be? Judging from the character of the verses we have examined thus far, an exploration of the Big Bang or any other creation theory will not satisfy the demands of this question. The second line of this verse points to the source of ignorance that leads to our misunderstanding of the world: the mind. Here in a few words is one of the most essential of spiritual principles: Everything is created in the mind.

15. Just as a clay pot, no matter the size or shape, is made of earth and nothing else, so are the many, one. The dream is created by thought, and these two together are the product of Reality, of pure Being. The two arise from the One. This is the reasoning called inquiry into truth.

15. Our dreams are created by mental activity. The dream would not exist without the substratum of the waking world which we think of as reality, and this world would not exist without the Awareness in which it appears, the underlying Reality that supports all the universes.

The word dream is used above, but it is often translated with words like illusion, delusion, or fantasy because, as we know, a dream is not real. The dream exists only in the mind. Similarly, as discussed in verse 14, the "real" world of our waking life can only be experienced as a result of our mental and perceptual activity. Shankara is telling us that both the world and our minds are dependent upon Reality, without which neither could exist. This Reality is existence itself, Existence with a capital E. It is the I Am that we feel at our very core; it is That which is the ground and cause of absolutely every form of dreaming that can come into being. It is Being.

This unnamable something is occasionally referred to as the "one without a second." Everything arises from it. Everything arises because of it. It is indescribable, inconceivable; it is absolute Reality. It is what Shankara and all the great teachers, past and present, would have us realize.

16. *I am the One. I am the knower, the imperishable witness. I am the ever-existent and unchanging Self, beyond body and mind. I am the I Am. This is the reasoning that results from inquiry into truth.*

16. The primordial question, "Who am I?," is answered here without qualification. In verse 13, Shankara says, "I am not this body nor this collection of senses; I am something different from these." Now he tells us what that "something" is.

Throughout our lives, we have identified ourselves as this body. We have automatically taken ourselves to be our thoughts and feelings. It did not make any sense to claim otherwise. How could we be anything *but* the things we think and feel? Yet here is Shankara, echoing the voices of an ancient wisdom, insisting that we are not what we think we are. We are *not* what we think.

The Experience of Reality

We are not the thinker of our thoughts. Who we are is altogether beyond the thinking mind. We are the *witness* of the thoughts that appear in the mind. Even the mind itself is only an appearance on the screen of Consciousness. There is a subtle essence about us that is always the same, an unchanging presence, no matter our moods or circumstances, and that Beingness that we feel is exactly what we are and all that we are; the true Self.

17. This Self is my very Being, an undivided whole. This body is composed of many parts, ever-changing and short-lived. To imagine that the body could be this infinite Self is evidence of a great misunderstanding.

17. Here begins a vigorous attempt to divest us of the conviction that we are this physical body which has been the source of our identity throughout our lives.

During the course of his repeated emphasis on our confusion of the body with the Self, Shankara showers us with knowledge about a deeper reality which lies just beyond our identification with the body. If we can muster the faith to trust these teachings, we will automatically relate to them with greater respect. More importantly, we can then embrace these new ideas (which are very old) as if they apply directly to us. Shankara and the *Upanishads* are not indulging in hypothetical supposition; they are making every effort to create the conditions that lead to the direct experience of Being, the experience of Reality.

18. The Self is the inmost Spirit, the ruler of the body. The body is external in every respect and entirely subject to the laws of nature. To mistake the body for the Self is the greatest ignorance.

18. Many texts refer to the individual self by assigning the word a lower case "s," whereas the universal Spirit, common to us all, employs the upper case "S". The use of the word "Self" in conjunction with Spirit can be misleading because of our

lifelong association of self with our bodies and personalities. As a result of this failure to distinguish the personal from the transpersonal, some of us begin to imagine that the personal "self" is the source and manifestation of divinity. This misunderstanding leads to confusion and discord, and it can substantially delay our recognition of our true identity.

For the vast majority of us, life revolves around an image of the body as the self, as who we are; and that self, no matter how expansively perceived, is necessarily the lower case self. The true Self is entirely beyond any personal qualities and is thus inconceivable in terms of our ordinary lives. The Self is the primordial witness; it is the heart of existence and so deeply felt that, in the beginning, most of us are unable to discern its presence. We are unable to feel the existence of the vast Self because it is so familiar, so much the heart of who we are that it is invisible to us. Just as the finger cannot point to itself nor the eye see itself, we are too close to see the seer, and thus we ignore or deny the one true thing. We *literally* look right through this simple Being that pervades each moment and yet goes unnoticed as the root cause of every experience. Ancient wisdom firmly declares that this basic Beingness is totally independent of the body. It is Reality. It is also known as the Self.

19. The Self is pure Consciousness and holy. The body is composed of flesh and fluids and subject to decay. How can the body be mistaken for the Self?

19. Here is another clear explanation of the subtle reality that is the Self. Shankara defines the Self as Consciousness, not consciousness of our identity or consciousness of the myriad objects of the world, but pure, ever-present Consciousness that exists prior to the appearance of objects. Perfect and self-luminous, Consciousness shines like the light that we cannot see except for the presence of tiny dust particles (objects) that make it visible. Consciousness always shines, whether objects are present or not; and That, Shankara tells us, is what we are.

The Experience of Reality

20.   The Self is the illuminator of the universe and purity itself. The body is the source of confusion and ignorance. To mistake the body for the Self is to be lost in that ignorance.

20.   The first sentence states Shankara's case perfectly; the second describes our predicament: we are the natural product of a lifetime of programming that keeps us deeply identified with this body-mind. Our minds are busy all day long with the affairs of the apparent lives being lived by our bodies, and the thoughts in our heads hold such power over us that we unwittingly believe ourselves to be what the thoughts tell us.

The body is the source of confusion and ignorance because the body is the source of thought. Thoughts, which run rampant in us all day, every day, are the source of all the confusion we experience. This confusion perpetuates ignorance by drawing our attention away from the direct experience of the present moment, and creating, in its place, ideas *about* the experience of the present moment. Just as often, we forsake the present moment altogether by indulging in thoughts about the past or the future, surrendering alternately to memory and imagination, each of which provides an absorbing diversion and perpetuates our estrangement from actuality.

For Shankara, our principal ignorance is the lack of awareness of our true identity. From ancient times into our present age, we have been hearing, and disregarding, the same timeless injunction: "Know Thyself." We have heard this directive repeated many times because it is so central to our true well-being and yet, we do not know how to respond. What does it mean to know oneself?

21.   The Self is pure Existence and timeless. The body is temporary and will soon cease to be. How can this body be mistaken for the Self?

21.   We can think of the injunction "Know Thyself" as our prime directive. What is this Self that we are being encouraged to know? Some say that the answer to this question effectively answers everything by allowing us to appreciate the relativity of

our questions when seen in the light of absolute Truth, the Truth of the Self.

In each of the last 5 verses, we are reminded that our true identity cannot be found in this temporary body. We might be tempted to take these verses lightly because we have already received this message, loud and clear. But in these verses, Shankara not only tells us what we are not, he tells us what we are. Rather than challenging us to decipher the truth from among a collection of hints and clues, he describes the qualities of the Self outright, at least to the degree that words permit:

Verse 17: The Self is "my very Being."
Verse 18: The Self is "the inmost Spirit."
Verse 19: The Self is "pure Consciousness."
Verse 20: The Self is "the Illuminator of the universe."
Verse 21: The Self is "pure Existence."

Shankara, in his compassion for our dilemma, offers us direct instruction. Now it is up to us. Can we bring ourselves to trust these words, not blindly, but by bringing inquiry and analysis to each statement? What is the Self? It is what we are. It is our being, our Existence. The Self is the This-ness that brings the taste of Reality to this moment. We do not simply exist in this moment, we *are* this moment. Everything that exists, exists in what we are, *because* we are, and this Being-ness is the Self.

The truth revealed here and is so deceptively simple that we must take care that it does not escape us. Our best chance to appreciate the value of these ideas is to examine them with an eye to our own mental processes which are, ultimately, the only obstacle to our direct experience of the Self. Mostly, we know only our mental processes, which we have long taken to be who we are. Shankara is encouraging us to notice, instead, the Consciousness in which all of our mental processes appear and disappear. What is this Self? It is this Being that is the totality of this moment. This very moment is entirely dependent upon the Self, upon Existence. Simple as This.

In the *Aparokshanubhuti* we are being offered a set of instructions designed to generate a radically new appreciation of what is finally true. Shankara has gathered all the elements necessary to bring this venture to fruition. The only additional ingredient called for in this recipe is an open mind.

From this point forward, commentaries will appear only occasionally. Shankara's words are very simple and direct; if we give these words careful consideration, they will reveal their riches.

22.   Everything in the universe is illumined by the light of Consciousness, which is the Self. Physical light cannot compare to the effulgence of the Self, which shines even in darkness.

23.   How strange that we temporarily inhabit this body and refer to it thus as, "my body," as if we possess it, the way we possess a pot or a cup, and yet we still imagine it to be who we are. This body is no different from any other object, and, like every object, it is limited, transitory, and not to be mistaken for the Self.

24.   I am not this physical body, which lasts for only a moment. I am the one Reality, changeless and quiescent, the cause of Being and the source of consciousness and bliss. Knowledge of this is the highest wisdom.

25.   Changeless am I, formless, immaculate, beyond space and time. How can I be this body which is never the same and subject to decay? This is called knowledge of the real.

26.   This Self is beyond imperfection, beyond illusion, beyond comprehension by the mind. The Self exists everywhere and pervades everything, whereas this body is doomed from the outset.

Aparokshanubhuti with commentary

27. *This body is under the control of all the laws of nature, and finally unreal. I am beyond all qualities, unconditioned, perpetual and ever-free. How could this body contain me?*

28. *The Self is without limits, imperishable, immovable, infinite and pure. The body is the very opposite of these qualities. How can I be that? This is called the knowledge of the wise.*

29. *Only the ignorant think the body is real and the spirit is not real. Do not make this mistake. The Self is the only reality. Do not be fooled by appearances. The Self pervades the body but is independent of it. The body is entirely dependent and relative.*

30. *Enough ignorance. We must come to know the Self. Study the scriptures and carefully and earnestly apply reasoning to this mystery. The Self is not a void. It is the source of our Existence and very difficult to see, hypnotized as we are by the body and the mind.*

31. *The supreme Self is One and the same in each of us. It can be detected by the sense of "I," common to us all. Our bodies are many while the Self is One. Why do we confuse them?*

32. *That which we call "I" is always the subject, while the body can only be an object of perception. When we refer to the body, we say, "This is my body." Why do we confuse the body with the Self?*

32. The body is external in every respect. It is perceived as separate from us even when inspected in the most intimate detail. Shankara reminds us that we say, "my hand, my eye, my brain." Never do we refer to any of these as "me," and yet we consider them collectively and declare them to be the only logical source

61

of our existence. Earnest inquiry into the nature of truth reveals the weakness in such logic.

33. From infant to elder, there is never a moment when our bodies are not changing. As the body transforms from child to adult, our ideas and understanding also change. But the Self never changes. Our bodies and minds may be in constant flux, but our true identity is timeless and unchanging.

34. Many are those wise ones who have discovered the secret of the Self through study of the scriptures. All the glories of the transcendental realms are inherent in this sublime Spirit, the one Self of all. How could this limited body contain the limitless Self?

35. Again and again the scriptures declare that the whole of manifest existence is the Self and nothing else. How could this body contain the universe?

35. That which we call the Self is pure Being-Awareness in which everything has its existence. Anything and everything, no matter how momentous, no matter how insignificant, is simply an appearance within this Self. The importance of this instruction lies in the potential for each of us to recognize its intimate relevance and to apply it to our own experience here and now. Reality, which is the ground and essence of all existence, is exactly *this* Awareness which is attending to these words. This Awareness, fully present and active right now, is the root cause and central fact of all existence.

36. The scriptures clearly state that the Self is beyond all conditions and limitations, pure and perfect. This body is bound at every turn by inescapable limitations; how could it be the condition-less Self?

37. The Self shines by its own light, infinite and independent. The earthbound body is lit only from without. If not for the light of the Self, the body would be completely inert. How can we imagine that the body is who we are?

38.   The most ancient scriptures, including those which prescribe rules for our behavior, declare that Spirit is different from the body and never ceases to exist, while the body will surely die, and soon. How can we confuse Spirit with the body?

39. Even the subtle energy body is composite and dependent. It is an ephemeral object of perception and therefore separate from the perceiver. Only the ignorant mistake the subtle body for the Self.

39. In every realm of existence, we are called upon to practice discrimination; to distinguish that which has a beginning from that which is beginningless. All "things" are relative things and are not to be confused with the Absolute about which nothing can be said.

40. The Self is, in fact, the transcendental Lord of the universe and also the personal God. We feel the Self within the physical and subtle bodies as the indwelling Spirit. I am that Spirit. I am the Self of all. I am all, imperishable and beyond all.

40. Many of us have difficulty relating to the powerful "I am" declarations that appear in nondualistic literature. Shankara identifies the Self as all and everything, and then goes on to declare that he is that Self. In some translations of this verse Shankara says, "I am Lord of the Universe."
    If we take such a statement from the conventional perspective of individual human beings who see ourselves as separate and distinct from one another, such a proclamation is the height of arrogance, a dangerous aberration, and an invitation for a mental health arrest. But Shankara is not referring to his physical self and its attendant personality. He has realized directly the truths that are set forth in the *Upanishads*, and he knows beyond any

doubt that the direct experience of the ultimate Oneness of everything leaves no room for a separate individual. There is only One, all things are One, and here "I am."

We will have an easier time accepting this enormous leap if we approach it from another angle. Rather than thinking, "I am All," we can hold the feeling "All is me."

All is one. These words are not just a lofty affirmation and a noble idea. It is a fact; it is *the* fact. Everything fits together in this One. There is no space left for anything other than the One. It must follow that we *are* this One, this Awareness that is experiencing these words in this moment. All is One, there is no second thing, no other Awareness. The One that is All is *this* One, this Awareness, shining as this moment.

41. To speak of the material body and to compare it to the Self might seem to lend some credibility to the body and to imply that the phenomenal world is real. But what purpose can be served by such thinking? The truth of our Being extends far beyond these fleeting appearances.

42. The body, gross and subtle, appears to exist only by the light of that Supreme Reality known as the Self. Listen now to the reasoning that dissolves all differences.

43. Reality is Oneness beyond division. This Oneness is manifest as Awareness, and all that appears to exist has its being in Awareness. The conception of every thought, the perception of every phenomenon, each and all are appearances on the screen of Awareness. Just as a rope can appear to be a snake, so can the supreme Self appear to be a separate self. It is appearance only.

44. Absence of knowledge of the rope is the immediate cause of the appearance of the snake. Absence of knowledge of pure Awareness is the immediate cause of the appearance of the body and the world.

44. The peace we are enjoying as we walk through the forest may come to an abrupt halt if we spy a length of rope lying in our path and mistake it for a snake. Thus the rope has two aspects, real and unreal; and so it is with everything. In reality, there is only Awareness, the timeless and changeless screen upon which the objects and events of the physical universe have their momentary existence, whether that existence extends over billions of years or begins and ends in the blink of an eye.

Everything that appears, appears in Awareness. Everything that appears in Awareness, disappears. Awareness always is. The wise, blessed with the ability to discriminate between the real and the unreal, appreciate the unreality of all appearances and are at peace, basking in the perpetual light of the Self.

45. The One, the Absolute, is the sole cause of the material universe. There is no second thing. It follows, therefore, that this entire universe is nothing other than ultimate Reality.

45. First we are told that the world is a dream. Now we are being told that the world is Reality. Which is it? Well, it is both, and neither, and beyond both; far beyond.

If we follow the reasoning of this verse, we can see that everything has its existence as a result of this Oneness. It is not as if there is ultimate Oneness floating in the void far beyond this physical universe. One means one. The void is also that One. Remember, everything has its being in Consciousness. Even the void is an appearance in Consciousness. So whatever appears in Consciousness is nothing other than supreme Being taking the shape of the perceived object. This means every wave of emotion we feel, every thought we think, every sound we hear, every person we see, every scrap of paper, every gust of wind, everything, is Spirit alone; Spirit which has taken form, and which always remains, in each moment, pure and infinite.

The Experience of Reality

Elsewhere, Shankara has written a statement that defines nondualism: "The World is an illusion, Brahman alone is real, Brahman is the world." Everything that appears to be, can only be a manifestation arising in that which is.

If there is only One, nothing can be separate. A unique consequence of this revelation is that *we* are One. This refers not simply to the totality of all of us, but it also means that each one of us, as an individual, is the One. Here is another opportunity to appreciate how dramatically these teachings differ from ordinary spiritual instruction. Here is a core principle of nondual wisdom; the meaning and natural consequence of "not two." We must eventually accept the fact that we are not simply a part of the whole. We are not a tiny constituent in the vastness of ultimate Reality; we *are* Reality. All is One. Each of us *is* that One. There is one Awareness and the Awareness that is attending to these words *is* that One Awareness. It is inescapable. There is only One. How could it not be who you are? How could it not be you?

46. The most holy of the scriptures declare that "All is One." All is this supreme Spirit, this pure Self, this ultimate Reality. There is no separate universe pervaded by the holy Spirit. The idea of the pervading and the pervaded is an illusion. There is only the One that is All. When we know this sacred Truth, how can we make distinctions? How can we see differences?

46. The world that appears in Awareness *is* Awareness and nothing else. The world that appears in Awareness is Spirit and nothing else. It is God, it is Consciousness and nothing else.

When the mind is still or quietly receptive, our physical and mental faculties begin to resonate with this underlying Reality that is the material cause of all the universes. This is the heart of spiritual practice. As we become attuned to the actuality of the One without a second, the truth contained in these verses begins to reveal itself in our day to day and moment to moment experience. Indeed, this single verse, if understood, would bring lasting peace to the world.

47.   The great scriptures uniformly deny any multiplicity or distinction in the Oneness of the Absolute. How then can we imagine that the phenomenal universe is anything other than this same Absolute?

48.   The scriptures decry the folly of seeing multiplicity in the part-less One. To see differences in the Undifferentiated is the height of calamity and necessarily leads to continued suffering.

49.   All beings are born from this One which is supreme Spirit. All beings, therefore, are this ultimate Reality and nothing else. Be convinced of this.

50.   The great scriptures insist that all apparent manifestations, all forms and the names that we assign to them, exist only within the underlying reality that is the Absolute. The many cannot exist except for the One.

51.   The essential nature of a gold ring is gold alone. If a gold ring is refashioned into a pendant, the essential nature of the pendant is gold. Whatever the appearance, the gold is unaffected; so also with the changeless Spirit. No matter the form of manifestation, immutable Spirit is One.

52.   If we forget that our essential nature is Spirit alone, if we think of ourselves as separate individuals, distinct from all other forms of creation, we are destined to feel the fear of extinction. If we know ourselves to be that One which is All, what is there to fear?

The Experience of Reality

53. When we forget our oneness with all that is, we begin to perceive the duality of subject and objects, of self and others; but when we remember our true identity as the changeless Self of All, the illusion of separation vanishes. There is always only One.

54. When we realize that all apparently separate persons, places, and things are that One Self which we always are, we find ourselves free from delusion and misery; duality dissolves into nonduality.

55. The great scriptures declare that the true Self, our own infinite Being, is exactly that supreme Self, that ultimate Reality, which is also the one Self of all and everything.

55. Many of us are uncomfortable with the use of the word "Self." Other terms like Spirit or Truth seem more appropriate for referring to absolute Reality. How can we pretend that we are equal to God or that the whole of existence is contained within us? We are naturally more comfortable with the concept of the individual self. After all, that is who we are, or who we seem to be. Our bodies, and the personal and private lives that we lead surely give the impression of a particular and unique self, unlike anyone else. We live our entire lives in, from, and through this body, this personality, this set of personal circumstances. How can this not be who we are?

Shankara tells us that we are not this body. This is especially difficult to accept because we are, at this moment, inarguably here in this body, reading these words. But Shankara has also told us that what we are, in reality, is Consciousness, which only appears to be located in this body. He reminds us that this body will not last long, and he assures us that who and what we are does not die when the body dies. This is not new information. Many of us were raised in cultural settings that assured us that our spirit lives on. But the rationale for this popular point of view requires cultivating a belief system that supports these promises. Shankara gives us much more than a simple assurance that we are not the body; he repeatedly tells us what we are *not*, so that we will be prepared for the revelation of what we are, and then leads us to the direct experience of that which does not die: Spirit, also referred to as the Self.

We may argue that our identity as the Self is no longer a surprise. We have already been informed that we are the ultimate and final truth of life; we are becoming accustomed to the idea. But the "idea" that we are pure Consciousness is not the point that Shankara is making. Those who know the truth of the Self can attest that even the most glorious *ideas* about reality can only be compared to the direct *experience* of Reality as one would compare the light of a campfire to the light of the sun.

The self that we seem to be is a temporary manifestation of this life that is going on all around us. The Self that we are in reality is the sum total of everything, and that means everything of which we are aware, and the infinitude that exists beyond our personal awareness. But this too, like life after death, seems to require a belief system. Shankara, in the company of the great wisdom teachers of the world, tells us that our true identity is nothing less than ultimate Reality, beyond all knowing and yet more real than any form of existence. Why should we believe these teachers? Granted, they seem to be telling us this purely for our own benefit, but aren't we just trading one set of beliefs for another? Maybe the ideas are more elevated than our previous notions, but should we simply take these ideas on faith? Shankara exclaims, No! and would urge us to recall the popular adage: "There is no substitute for experience."

The title of Shankara's book, created specifically for our benefit, is translated variously into English as *Direct Experience of Reality, Self-Realization, Intimate Experience of Reality, Direct Cognition of the Unity of Self and Reality,* and *Direct Experience of I-Am.* These titles leave no doubt that the subject matter of the *Aparokshanubhuti* is not a theoretical investigation of the principles of a nondual philosophy. The terms "intimate experience" and "direct cognition" indicate that the theme of this book is not a matter of mere conjecture but an experiential opportunity. Our job is to discover for ourselves whether these assertions are true. Indeed, as the title suggests, the proof of Shankara's words is available for our direct experience by careful consideration of the radical ideas contained within his book.

The word radical may conjure up images of outrageous ideas and intellectual anarchy, but the root of the word radical is, appropriately, "root." Radical means going to the source, to the origin. Radical means fundamental and it means essential. So it follows that the revolutionary nature of the word radical is entirely appropriate in this context, for these ancient ideas are drastically different from the ordinary ways most of us think about spirituality, even if we are well-versed in the subject. There is no amount of intellectual understanding that can compare to the fruits of direct experience.

56. This world, though an object of our daily experience and serving practical purposes, is a dream-world. The dream we dream at night seems real until we wake, and our waking life seems real until we dream again. The world of our waking life is of the same order of experience as the dream world.

56. If the events we experience in our dreams were resumed each night right where we left off the previous morning, how would those experiences differ from what we think of as our waking life? Indeed, if we are no more able to recall our waking life during the dream state than we are to recall our dream life during our waking state, it is only the continuity of the waking state that makes it seem more real.

We may argue that the dream state is much less tied to the laws of nature and thus less real than the waking state, but does it seem so when we are actively dreaming? Situations and events that seem impossible in our waking state are commonplace within the dream and are only called into question from the perspective of our waking life, as when we recall a vivid dream and describe it as strange and surreal. Is there anyone among us who has not said or, at least, thought, "I had a weird dream last night."?

Even this physical universe, our natural-world home in the waking state, this world that seems so unquestionably real, has been revealed to be a fabrication composed of unimaginably tiny and distant particles which are comprised of essentially nothing at all. But it seems so real!

It is not useful to simply declare that the world is unreal and expect this bizarre claim to be accepted on faith, especially when everything about our waking experience tells us otherwise. But Shankara's teaching is informed by direct insight into the nature of Reality, a knowledge beyond the experience of the thinking mind. Joining the voices of the great spiritual seers of antiquity, he agrees that our dream-life only seems real until we awaken, and then goes on to assure us that, in exactly the same way, our earthly life only seems real until we awaken.

Shankara does not expect us to take his word for it; he instructs us to look and see for ourselves. He provides a set of rational indicators intended to lead us to a state of transcendental insight, a state of being that is beyond the relativities of space and time.

Our daily business-as-usual life makes it all the more difficult to appreciate the dreamlike qualities of our waking life. Many times an insight into our waking dream-state takes the form of a rude awakening. In these circumstances, our awareness of the dream may appear as a waking nightmare, such as during life and death struggles that may accompany accidents or sudden illness. Death of a less immediate nature, like terminal illness and even normal aging, can also find us feeling the surreal qualities of a life and a world that is out of our control. Sadly, one of the situations most likely to spark this awareness can be found in the living nightmare of wartime.

Of course, glimpses into the dreamlike nature of our lives are not caused only by negative experiences. Any abrupt and dramatic change in our lives may make us feel as if we are dreaming. Landmark events such as weddings, graduations, funerals, winning the lottery, or being present at a birth can be potent triggers for such an experience.

57. When we are awake, the dream state does not exist. When we are dreaming, the waking state does not exist. Both dreaming and waking disappear in the deep sleep state, which, in turn, cannot exist in the waking or dreaming states.

The Experience of Reality

58. Thus, all three states are not ultimately real. They, like all phenomena, are the result of the play of elements and qualities which, also, in the end, are without enduring reality. But the witness of all these states is timeless Being-Awareness. Everything that comes into existence is destined to pass away. Only the beginningless is endless.

58. Everything in the universe, including the universe itself, comes into being and exists for a period of time. Some elementary particles exist for infinitesimal fractions of a second while stars exist for billions of years. But even stars are physical entities and subject to the limitations of a relative existence; their "days" are numbered.

But what is aware of this? What, for that matter, is aware of anything? In the midst of a world undergoing constant transformation, what is it that is conscious of this constant change? The answer? Awareness! And that, say the great wisdom teachings, is exactly what we are, pure Being-Awareness, free of any sense of identity and beyond relationship of any sort, because nothing is separate from what we are. All things are the same thing and we are That.

Once we have realized that our true identity is composed entirely of this Being-Awareness, then all the mysteries that confound us dissolve like the morning dream from which we awaken into the real life that is always, already here.

59. We might look at an exquisite piece of mother-of-pearl and imagine that it contains pure silver. After all, it appears to be even more perfectly silver than real silver. Sometimes we look at a beautiful pottery vase and imagine it to be something other than the clay from which it is made. Sometimes we look at ourselves and imagine that we are something other than supreme Spirit which is, in fact, all that we are.

60. Just as a vase is only clay, the apparent silver is only mother-of-pearl, and a ring is nothing but gold, so is that which we call "myself" nothing other than the supreme Self of All, the One Reality. The appearance of an individual with a name and form and a separate existence is only a fleeting dream, soon to disappear.

61. The blueness in the sky, the mirage in the desert, the form of a person superimposed upon a distant post, all illusions. So too is this universe taken to be separate from the One Self.

61. Walking in the twilight we may look into the distance and see a post or the stump of a tree and imagine it to be a person. Walking in the desert, we look across the landscape and perceive a mirage. If we have no knowledge of mirages, we are likely to imagine that we see water. We look into the sky and it is very clearly blue. But the sky is not blue, it only appears to be blue. We look into the mirror and think that what we see is who we are.

Take a moment to feel the sensation of looking at our image in the mirror. What do we really feel about ourselves in that moment? If we get beyond our observations and judgments about our reflected image and the history we attribute to it, we may discover that what we feel, all that we feel, is the sensation of seeing, the sensation of being that which is looking.

If we experience this seeing directly, without identification or interpretation of the object that is seen, we can readily feel this Awareness that Shankara has been commending to us all along. This Awareness with which we see the image in the mirror is exactly the same great Awareness in which *everything* appears. This Awareness is the ground and essence of this moment. This is why we find it so difficult to understand Awareness. We think it is something other than what we already are. Imagine our surprise when we realize that This Awareness which is happening right now is the only enduring Reality.

The Experience of Reality

62   Just as a ghost may appear in empty space, or we might see an animal or a castle in the clouds; just as, when our eyes relax, we might see two moons in the sky, so does this universe appear before us. The universe appears because of the existence of Reality, which is also known as Consciousness and as the Self.

62. Reality is precisely this ever-present Awareness in which all things appear. In actual fact, there are not two things, so that one thing can see the other. We can never see the source of this seeing because there is only one thing and we are It. Consider this simple fact deeply for it is the doorway to the experience of Reality.

63.   A wave upon the ocean, no matter its shape or size, is made entirely of water. A copper vessel, no matter its shape or size, is made entirely of copper. This universe and every individual thing in this universe, no matter its shape or size, is made entirely of that nameless One that is the ground and cause of everything.

64.   Just as it is clay alone that appears as the many kinds of pottery, or thread alone that takes the name of cloth, so is it Consciousness alone that is referred to as the world. When we see beyond names and forms, we find the underlying Reality, the Truth that always is.

65.   Every single thing that happens in this world and in our lives, happens in and through this supreme Spirit, without which there would be nothing whatsoever. Millions of pieces of pottery fill our homes and marketplaces. They are not pots, jars, vases, bowls, cups, and mugs and pitchers, they are all made of one thing. They may appear to be different, but they are all the same.

66. *An earthen jar will never exist but for the clay from which it is made. Just so, this universe, and this self that we take ourselves to be, could not exist except for the existence of Reality which supports all appearances. Supreme Being is beyond cause; It gives rise to all the universes.*

67. *Every thought of the earthen jar includes an awareness of the earth through which it has its being. Sometimes the awareness is subtle, sometimes obvious and central to our appreciation of the vessel. It is the same with our awareness of the beginningless and ever-shining Spirit that underlies our every experience. We may not notice it, but it is always here; the only true and lasting part of the existence that we think of as "this life."*

68. *The rope is always a rope, it is never a snake. Though Awareness is pure and perfect, it appears to the ignorant as imperfect because we see only the world of objects and not the Self which is the cause of the world.*

69. *Just as the jar is nothing but earth, so is this body nothing but Consciousness, nothing but Spirit; so is this world only Awareness, only Spirit, the One Self. When we create such distinctions as "this is self" and "that is not self," we have missed the Oneness that is present in and as everything. Indeed, All is One.*

70. *To the hard-headed materialist, the body and the world are the only reality. When we see things in this way, the rope is always a snake and every mirage sends us scurrying after the illusion of water, or security, or happiness, none of which can be found in a mirage.*

The Experience of Reality

71. We see a beautiful clay pot and forget that it is nothing but earth. We hold a fine piece of clothing and forget that it is only thread. Unravel the thread and where is the cloth? So it is with that which we see in the mirror; remove the reality of the indwelling Spirit, our true and only identity, and where and of what use is the body, and who is there to see it?

72. We admire the glistening earring and forget that it is only gold. We watch the endless waves rolling in and forget that it is only water. We become hypnotized by the apparent drama in our lives and forget that all of it is Spirit dancing on the surface of the ocean of Existence.

73. A post in the distance is mistaken for a person. It is not a person, it is a post. A mirage appears to be water. It is not water, it is a mirage. The physical body, the face we see in the mirror, is thought to be our true identity. But the body is a dependent reality and not the final truth. Remember, there is only One.

74. A pile of timber may be assembled into a house, but the house is only wood. A heap of metal may be fashioned into a sword, but the sword is nothing but metal. The deathless Spirit takes on the appearance of a body and mind, but at no time is the apparent body-mind anything but pure Spirit.

75. We stand at the edge of the pond and see the nearby trees reflected on the surface of the water. We see the image of the tree, but it is only water. We look at ourselves and see and feel a body-mind, but it is only an image projected on the surface of Consciousness.

76. *When we stand on the deck of a ship as it moves up river, we seem to be standing still and everything along the banks appears to be in motion. Similarly, we imagine that our bodies are moving through this busy world when in reality our true identity is stillness itself, ever-present Spirit, and life unfolds in this timeless Being-Awareness .*

77. *For a person suffering from jaundice, every white object appears to be yellow. When we do not understand the truth of the Self, every object we see appears to be real and we imagine that the body is who we are.*

78. *To the nearsighted person, the world is blurry and indistinct. Just so, when we have not recognized the Self, we are not able to see things as they really are. We feel the presence of the Self and think that it is the body.*

78. We think that the body is the source of the Self and we imagine that we are dependent upon the world for our existence. In reality, it is the other way around: everything is dependent for its existence upon the Awareness in which it appears. Without Awareness, which is the Self, nothing is.

79. *We pull a firebrand from the flames and whirl it into the appearance of a fiery circle. But there is no circle of fire; there is only a point of light. We assume an identity upon our birth into this world and soon find our lives whirling through a circle of events. But it only appears to be a circle of events; all phenomena are nothing but timeless Awareness, the source of this universe and this moment.*

80. *Just as a grand and inspiring object, when seen at a distance, appears to be small and insignificant, so too, without true Knowledge, does the infinite Self appear to be as small and insignificant as the physical body.*

The Experience of Reality

80. The direct experience of our identity as infinite Being is the key to real Knowledge. Even a momentary glimpse of this boundless perfection gives rise to an immediate appreciation of all relative things, including the recognition that *all* things are relative.

The rumor of some distant Absolute, far away and attainable only by the select few, is replaced by the conviction that there is nothing real standing between us and uninterrupted peace, no matter how challenging our outer circumstances may be. This body, which once seemed to be our totality, is recognized as too limited to encompass what we know ourselves to be.

We have always imagined God, or Reality, to be something unattainable, something that we contemplate or worship, but clearly something that is forever above and beyond us. Now we discover that Reality is much closer than we thought. Reality, it turns out, is not out there and apart from us: it is right here. It is nothing other than this very Awareness, the knowingness that we are in this moment. This Awareness is the real part, the only real part, of this life that we are living. The ultimate Truth, the God we tried so desperately to imagine, does not abide at a distance; Reality is more real than that. Reality is so close that we cannot see it; we cannot see it because we *are* It.

81. We are only able to acknowledge the existence of tiny waterborne creatures after they have been made visible to us with the use of a lens. So too, without direct experience, we are reluctant to concede the existence of an ultimate Consciousness and thus we continue to insist that the body is who we are.

82. In the distance, we glimpse a pane of glass lying in the road and mistake it for a puddle of water. Looking more closely, we can see the truth. When we are born into the pleasures and pains associated with this body, we naturally take it to be the only reality. On closer inspection, often prompted by the words of the wise, we may see beyond our first impressions and recognize the Reality behind the appearance.

83. *If we were to happen upon a glowing ember on the path, it might appear to us as a lost ruby. Similarly, if we were to see a lost ruby lying on the pathway, we might mistake it for a glowing ember. In either case, closer inspection would reveal the truth. If we were to inspect ourselves more closely, we would discover that this body is merely an object of awareness, while the Self is that Awareness.*

84. *When the clouds are moving swiftly, the moon seems to be running through the sky, and yet we know that the moon does not move so rapidly. We can tell the difference between appearance and reality. Yet when the body is busy and the mind is full, we are unable to recognize the stillness of the Self that is always present, supporting our every thought and deed.*

85. *We are hiking through the woods. We decide to leave the trail and take a shortcut. A few minutes later, we slip in the leaves and fall to the ground. When we finally get to our feet we realize that, without the path to guide us, we have become disoriented. It may take a few moments before we are able to get our bearings. It could take much longer. If we continue to insist that this body is who we are, we could be lost for a lifetime.*

86. *Reflected in still water, the image of the moon is still. When the wind disturbs the surface of the water, the image of the moon becomes distorted. When the clear light of Consciousness is reflected in an agitated mind, the world takes on a confusing appearance; the unreal is mistaken for Reality. Just as the moon is untouched by the changeful nature of wind and water, so Awareness is always shining, unaffected by the movements of the mind.*

The Experience of Reality

87. The body and the world appear to be real until the Self is directly experienced. Once the Self, the Truth of Awareness, has come to light, the conviction "I am the body" naturally dissolves.

87. It is the rare person who spontaneously awakens to the fact that every experience of their lives happens exclusively within the domain of Awareness and nowhere else. It is, in fact, rare to have the good fortune even to be exposed to the *idea* that everything arises in Awareness. The Awareness being discussed here is exactly *this* Awareness that is the entirety of this moment. Awareness *is* this moment.

This Awareness that is this moment and makes this moment real is also known as Spirit, as true life, and as the Self. The Eastern scriptures repeatedly refer to this Awareness as the Self because this Being-Awareness is the core of every experience and the source of our certainty that, whatever else may or may not be true, there is no doubt that "I Am."

It sounds too simple to be the whole story, but this sense of I Am, this pristine feeling of Being, is what is referred to by the word Self and by the word Spirit. If we bring ourselves into stillness and directly experience this Awareness, this Beingness, we find that we cannot truly see it, we can only *be* It. Resting in this intimate Being, we realize that we *are* It. This is the experience of Reality.

The experience of Reality is not blinding white light and celestial choirs; it is the direct and immediate recognition of this Being-Awareness, active at this very moment, as the root of life, the source and substance of everything.

88. When the whole of the universe, animate and inanimate, is known to depend for its existence upon the Self, the Reality of Awareness, where is the justification for imagining the physical body to be the Self?

89. Oh, You Intelligent One, who are drawn to these words; attend to them. Give yourself to contemplation of this supreme Wisdom which is the highest good of all beings and the ultimate purpose of every life. The vagaries of destiny are of no importance for one who lives in the knowledge of the One Spirit also known as the Self.

90. Many scriptures contend that one remains subject to the consequences of one's past actions until the debt has been paid, even though one should be otherwise liberated through direct knowledge of the Self. This view is hereby refuted.

90. The consequences of our actions are understood to have an impact on our lives. This idea is common to the majority of religious and philosophical observations about how life works. We know this concept variously as cause and effect, the law of karma, justice, final judgment, or just deserts. Sometimes we detect the results of our words or actions within minutes, hours, or days, or we may recognize the fruits of our actions long after the fact. When significant circumstances arise in our lives, be they negative or positive, rare is the person who has not thought, "I wonder what I did to deserve this?"

Shankara wants to ensure that we understand how differently the world looks to us once we realize that we are *not* the individual body-mind. Instead, we are this Consciousness, pure and simple. Once we recognize this Awareness in which all individual things and events appear, our habitual identification with the activities of the body and the thoughts of the mind diminishes. The body and mind continue to operate normally, but more naturally now, as we have ceased to try to control or identify with the spontaneous activities of the body-mind. Instead, we find ourselves resting in infinite Being.

This does not mean that, because we have seen beyond, we are no longer a part of our world, or that we become detached or insincere in our relationships. On the contrary; the body-mind that we heretofore felt ourselves to be, is now freed from the constraints of the ego. We find that every aspect of life is now lived more fully. We see more clearly, act more effectively, feel

81

more strongly, care more deeply, love more completely. We remain who we always were, but now we are free from the need to identify with the infinite particulars of this life. We are wholeness itself; we are a spacious presence in which every moment of life happens by itself, spontaneously, naturally.

We are the Self, changeless and infinite; we are the pure light of Awareness that illuminates everything and yet remains unaffected by the circumstances of the ever-changing world. When the reflection of the moon is disturbed by ripples in the water, the moon is not affected. Far beyond the dark clouds and heavy rain that turn day to night, the sun is always there. It is not dependent upon another sun for its illumination; it shines with inner light and makes everything visible. Just so is the Self.

The world is in constant flux and circumstances alter with each passing moment, but the changeless Self is prior to space and time; It existed before "we" were born, before the universe was born. Absolute Reality is beyond even the ultimate relativities of being and not-being. It cannot be approached by mere thought. Only direct experience can reveal the Truth.

91. When the sleeper awakes, the dream disappears. When we detect and recognize the self-luminous light of Awareness, we immediately understand the relativity and impermanence of the world of appearances. The body is known to be an illusion and destiny is rendered meaningless. We are the One Self of All and this mental organism is a dream from which we are soon to awaken.

92. Many are they who point to the effects of past actions and insist upon the reality of reincarnation. But for those who have realized their identity as the unborn and deathless Spirit, such notions are no more real than last night's dream.

93. Just as the dream body is superimposed upon the mind, so is the physical body appearance only and ultimately unreal. How can such a temporary thing as this body be thought to be born into eternal life? The timeless Self exists before and after the body.

93. Both waking and dream states are superimposed upon Consciousness. During the time of dreaming, there is no question about the reality of the body that is ours for the duration of the dream, and yet upon waking we recognize its unreality. While we are dreaming, it is rare that there is a question about whether we are awake or asleep. In the waking state, it is also rare that we ever question whether we are awake or asleep. We naturally assume that we are awake.

Many of us in the West are familiar with the deceptively meaningful childhood song, "Row, row, row your boat." If we heartily embrace the wisdom of the last line, "Life is but a dream," everything changes. Only when we awaken into this Awareness which contains *all* states of being, will we realize what it means to be truly awake.

94. The greatest scriptures declare the unreality of the phenomenal world and point to the indescribable Absolute as the ultimate Truth. The world as we know it exists only in the absence of this supreme Knowledge.

95. The rope in our path is always and forever a rope. It can never be a snake, no matter how deluded and convinced we may become. The world that we live in, that appears to us to be so real, is always and forever changeless Spirit alone.

95. Because of our conditioning, we project a pluralistic universe upon the field of Awareness and then seek ways to free ourselves from imagined limitations. All the while, we are always and entirely nothing but Consciousness, which we feel as the sense of " I Am."

The Experience of Reality

The many forms and phenomena that make up our world seem so real to us that it takes a powerful wake-up call to stir our suspicions about the "real world." Shankara is literally grabbing us by our concepts and shaking us out of a lifelong trance. This world, he reminds us, is composed of tiny particles, separated by enormous distances and composed of essentially nothing at all. The only reliable, permanent, unchanging Reality we can depend upon is this timeless Witness of all appearances. Behind all our thoughts and feelings, prior to everything we have imagined ourselves to be, lies Reality, Truth absolute, That which alone is.

96. When we realize that the snake in our path is only a rope, the illusion disappears in an instant, just so, when the Absolute is recognized, all separate things dissolve into the nameless One.

97. When it is finally acknowledged that the world and the universe which contains it are not ultimately real, it follows that the body, which is contained in the world, is also not real. It is only for those who identify with their bodies and their thoughts that teachings are provided regarding destiny and the fruits of action.

98. When one realizes the nondual Truth of Existence, one is immediately freed from the web of the world. The life of the individual soul becomes an appearance only, no more real than any other dream.

98. To be freed from the web of the world means to recognize the truth of nonduality. Stated simply, there are not two. There is no distinction between apparent things. The existence of the interdependent pairs of opposites rises and sets in the dream of two-ness. There can be no up without down, no positive without negative, no subject without object. When the infinite objects of the universe are recognized as mere projections on the screen of Consciousness, our identification of ourselves as a separate

consciousness also dissolves and there exists only the One Radiance shining out of Itself.

99. If, however, even after careful reasoning, we still cling to the idea of a separate self, we risk becoming embroiled in the absurdity of disagreeing with the holy teachings and thereby diminishing the possibility of being liberated in this lifetime. For if we refuse to embrace the nondual conclusion of divine Truth, we are condemned to a merely relative existence, bound irrevocably by the pairs of opposites.

100. Now are to be expounded the fifteen steps necessary for the attainment of direct knowledge of Reality. With the help of these guides, one should practice profound meditation upon the Holy Truth at all times.

100. We have established the existence of supreme Truth and we have acknowledged the possibility of its direct cognition. What follows now, beginning in verses 102 and 103, is the enumeration and explanation of fifteen steps of practice whereby we may realize this incomparable Knowledge. These steps, when embraced and practiced with faithfulness and constancy, will lead to the Knowledge that the Self is not an individual entity, separate and distinct, but rather the witnessing Awareness that is common to each of us, the One Self of all.

101. Without constant and steady practice, one cannot hope to realize that Reality which is the source of the life force and is, in fact, Awareness Itself. Therefore one must be earnest and persistent in the practice of meditation upon this infinite Truth.

101. This verse prepares us for the delineation of the fifteen steps by emphasizing the most important aspect of spiritual practice. It is very well to enjoy the study of these exalted ideas, but there is much more at stake here than intellectual enrichment. These teachings are not presented as an alternative philosophy

by which we may relate to the world from a more informed perspective. This teaching is not speculative.

The nondual principles that are introduced here represent the furthermost reaches of the human mind, pointing to levels of knowing well beyond the scope of thought. If we wish to participate in this rare and magnificent adventure, we must give ourselves to it with all the vigor and enthusiasm that we would apply to any wholehearted effort. Considering these towering concepts in our spare time or for twenty minutes once or twice a day will certainly lead to positive results, but it is less likely that such a relationship to the Absolute will result in the direct knowing that Shankara is urging upon us. The realization of this highest truth requires day-in and day-out, moment to moment dedication.

Only when we comprehend the magnitude of these teachings will we find ourselves earnestly drawn to these practices. Once we have begun to taste the fruits of the steps outlined here, our enthusiasm will surely intensify as we become ever more deeply convinced of the truth of these ancient words written solely for our benefit.

In the next two verses Shankara will tell us how we can go about discovering for ourselves the truths set forth in the first part of this book.

102-103. The following fifteen steps can lead to the Direct Experience of Reality. The steps are: control of the senses, control of the mind, renunciation, silence, space, time, posture, control of the nervous system, equilibrium, firmness of vision, control of the vital forces, withdrawal of the mind from the objects of sense, concentration, contemplation of the Self, and absorption. We will now examine these steps in order and consider the deeper meaning of each.

102-103. While there may appear to be an obvious sequential relationship between some of these "steps," they should not be thought of as ascending increments by which one climbs the stairway to heaven. This becomes clear as we proceed through these steps, for we discover that in each step Shankara urges us to do only one thing.

Shankara is not telling us that we must learn to control our relationship to our senses before we can learn to control the unruliness of our minds, after which we will be ready to practice renunciation, and only then will we finally be able to undertake the practice of silence. These are not truly "steps" along a path, nor are they stages that we must pass through. These are means, measures, methods.

Shankara has told us how things are, what things are, and what is the truth of life. But these ideas may be so new and unfamiliar that they are difficult to accept. So Shankara says, 'I have already told you the truth, but do not take my word for it, find out for yourselves! If you want to know the truth, here are steps you can take. Here are the means for coming to this understanding.'

Now we begin to examine the steps, the means. Right away we will see that Shankara is not indulging our predilection for translating his instructions into relative terms that we can understand. In every step we are denied the luxury of our literal interpretations and prompted instead to focus upon the Absolute.

104. The restraint of the senses is not the product of refusing to see and hear and think and feel, but rather to constantly hold the conviction that "all of this is God."

104. Immediately, Shankara challenges our preference for dualistic interpretations of popular spiritual instruction, and just as immediately, we can appreciate the grand design he intends. Rather than attempt to resist and overcome the natural tendencies of the mind and body, we are encouraged to bypass altogether the traditional methods of controlling the senses. Instead, we fix our gaze entirely beyond the realm of the senses. We do this by cultivating an ongoing acknowledgement that whatever sense-object appears in Consciousness, be it a thought or a thing, it comes into existence as a temporary manifestation arising in timeless Awareness. As Shankara puts it, "All of this is God."

The Experience of Reality

All is One. Every object of thought or sensation that appears in Consciousness *is* this One. So it is not necessary to turn away from the senses, but merely to recognize them for what they are, manifestations of this great Singleness. When that which others take to be a snake is known to be a simple piece of rope, the "snake" is imagination only, arising in the One.

The control of the senses as a spiritual practice is ubiquitous among wisdom traditions around the world. In the yogic system this approach was codified by Patanjali, a popular Indian teacher who is thought to have lived around the second century BCE. He organized and systematized some of the most traditional of the yogic practices. *The Yoga Sutras of Patanjali* is considered by many, East and West, to be the definitive word on the practice of yoga. Patanjali divided the practice of yoga into the eight limbs of Ashtanga Yoga which also became well-known as Raja Yoga, the royal yoga.

The first of these eight limbs, yama, is addressed in verse 104. Yama is external control, the restraint of behavior, the development of will-power. Divided into five parts, Yama is referred to as "Thou shalt not:" non-injury or non-violence, truthfulness in thought and deed (not lying to oneself or others), non-covetousness, self-restraint, temperance or abstinence, and non-possessiveness. Although laudable qualities and consistent with making progress along a spiritual path, Shankara takes issue with the reinforcement of an image of ourselves as separate persons who need to overcome a long list of imperfections. This effort toward self-perfection, in Shankara's view, fuels the illusion that we are isolated individuals traveling a path from duality and delusion to eventual union with God. In Reality, there is always only One and we can never be apart from our own infinite Being. If we believe otherwise, we are simply mistaken.

Here we find ourselves face to face with a decisive moment in our spiritual life. If we are to realize what Shankara intends, we must relinquish our sense of being a person who is on a spiritual path. As long as we see ourselves as separate, we are destined to travel a lengthy and arduous path of advancement and relapse as we inch our way toward a state of Oneness. Shankara wants us to realize that our separate self is a complete illusion. This realization happens immediately upon recognizing the true nature of our experience: the only thing we know for sure is our own Awareness, our Being, prior to any content. The contents of Awareness are always open to question, but Awareness itself is beyond question. The final Truth is, in fact, completely impossible to see, except in the direct experience of the Beingness that we always are. Before feelings, before concepts, before perception of any kind, *we are*; and That, says Shankara, is not something that requires any effort.

Patanjali's eight-limbed yoga is one of many methods that have come into existence to help us along the path from the temporal to the eternal. Shankara's revolutionary response to tradition asks, 'How can we follow a path to where we already are?' To advance from the temporal to the eternal still finds us in the grip of time, while ultimate Reality is timeless. Forever exists in the mind, not in Reality; there is only This.

Shankara tells us that the adoption of any path reinforces the mistaken notion that there is somewhere else we should be, that we are somehow separate from our true nature and that we must undergo a transformation in order to become what we truly are. He has already pointed out that we are not the body. Now he asks us to consider whether a philosophy that assumes that we are distinct individuals in need of improvement can help us realize that we are not individuals at all. We are this Awareness that is the source of this moment.

In our ordinary day-to-day state of consciousness, it is practically impossible to overcome the clamor of the mind and senses. The sights and sounds of the wide world, and the thoughts and feelings of the natural mind will be present for as long as we are alive. But Shankara encourages us to recognize the source of the world, notice how all things appear and disappear on the screen of Consciousness; feel the Being that brings everything into existence and know that all of it is This Awareness, ablaze in this timeless moment, always right now.

Shankara tells us that we need not struggle to turn away from the senses but rather encourages us to simply turn *toward* the core of our Being, this ever-present Awareness also known as the Self. From here, everywhere we look we see only the One.

The Experience of Reality

In the coming verses, Skankara addresses Patanjali's injunctions, and interprets each of them with a single message: Everything is the same thing; see all as One and be free from seeking and sorrow.

105. To cultivate and perpetuate a unitive thought such as "Only Consciousness is real" or "All is One," to the exclusion of all other kinds of thought, is known as control of the mind. The recognition of the light of Awareness as one's true Identity brings the very highest happiness. This the wise practice with diligence.

105. Here is the second of Patanjali's eight limbs; Niyama, inner control, the ability to keep the mind in equilibrium. Traditionally, Niyama consists of ten observances, of which Patanjali enumerates five. These are also referred to as the "Thou Shalt" of yoga: inner and outer purification (mind, body, deeds), contentment, self-discipline or austerity, study of the scriptures, and surrender to God. Again, as with Yama, these are all valuable activities resulting in beneficial consequences. Shankara, however, encourages a single activity which will result in the attainment of all the advantages available from the cumulative effects of the eight limbs of Raja Yoga. Indeed, each of the fifteen steps that Shankara enumerates in this treatise consists of the fundamental recognition of our true Self as This Being-Awareness in which every objective thing rises and sets.

106. True renunciation does not consist in turning one's back on the things of the world, but in seeing every object of perception as Awareness alone. When Reality dawns, illusions disappear, attachments fall away without aversion or effort, and things are seen as they are.

106. Here we can appreciate the radical nature of Shankara's perspective, which challenges one of the most cherished hallmarks of spiritual development. The traditional practice of renunciation requires that we strive to renounce greed, anger,

hatred, jealousy, covetousness, fear, prejudice, distraction, judgment, distrust of others, laziness, anxiety, lust for sense pleasures, doubts, desires, and attachments of every kind.

Shankara's nondualistic approach calls for us to renounce the notion of separateness. Here we experience everything as one thing, constantly reminding ourselves that the one thing is Awareness, *this* Awareness, in which everything happens.

In Shankara's view, the myriad renunciations of popular spiritual discipline are condensed into the steadfast refusal to see anything as separate from the Self, understanding that the Self is nothing other than this Awareness that is both the cause and the essence of everything. Everything that happens, happens in this timeless Awareness, the final Reality of each apparent moment.

When we live in this way, life lives itself; things and events unfold naturally, desires diminish, attachments weaken, and obstacles are seen as opportunities. Peace and contentment, no longer dependent upon circumstances, shine out of this timeless instant.

107. Even when speaking, the wise should always strive to be one with that Great Silence from which words, together with the mind, turn back, baffled by its perfection. This is the practice of silence.

107. Behind and before every thought that arises lies this Great Silence. Every word materializes out of silence. If we undertake the practice of stillness, this Great Silence is gradually revealed to us as we tune out the noise of the outside world, and, keeping our attention focused on stillness, allow the inner noise of our busy subjective world to subside.

Steeped in silence, we feel its presence in each moment, no matter what is happening in the objective world; and from this silence comes the peace that is said to surpass understanding.

The Experience of Reality

108. Who can describe That Supreme Spirit from which words turn away? Even the phenomenal world is beyond description, how much more so the Realm of the Absolute? When nothing can be said, what is there to say?

109. That state of being which is beyond expression gives birth to true silence which naturally arises when there are no adequate words. The mere restraint of speech is prescribed only for those who cannot approach stillness in the real way.

110. By the practice of place is meant abidance in the solitude of pure space, where neither thought nor the universe ever began or existed. From this place where nothing is, all things appear. The universe is born of this Reality.

110. Conventional spiritual practice recommends that we find or create an appropriate place in which to practice our spiritual disciplines. In this verse, Shankara expounds a radically new interpretation of "place." His approach to cultivating the experience of Reality has little use for those customary spiritual disciplines embraced and practiced by most seekers. We are traditionally instructed to find a quiet location to which we may retreat so as not to be disturbed during the performance of physical, mental and spiritual exercises. The ideal place is one that remains constant, so that we can develop a routine and schedule, and then adhere to time and place as closely as possible in order to bring a rhythm and harmony into our practice. If it is not possible to develop such a routine, we are encouraged to come as close as possible by locating a place that is free from distraction, and conducive to a successful effort. Even if our lifestyle dictates that we be in a different place every day, we are encouraged to keep to a consistent schedule and cultivate uniformity in our practice.

This pursuit of the proper environment for our practice assumes that we need a place to be, as if the location of the body is important to spiritual pursuits. Shankara calls us to the place of space, the place where nothing is. This is a place prior to every

92

individual thing, where even this universe has no independent existence. Even we, who undertake this practice, disappear into this place of pure space. Shankara reminds us that there is only One Place, One Space. All is One. Shankara will continually hold up this precious truth for us. The practice of place is *this* place, right here, right now, this spacious Awareness, the ground of Being. We are never, and can never be, anywhere but this place. There is only one place and we are it.

111. Timeless Reality is prior to all existence; it is manifest as Awareness of the universe as it appears in the blink of an eye and disappears in another blink. This is known as the practice of time.

111. The dream that constitutes our waking life is the result of supreme Being. Without That which is prior to everything, nothing can be, and because of That which always is, everything is.

The world that appears before us *is* time. Time and the world are not two separate phenomena. The practice of time is the conscious appreciation of the manifest universe as a mere glimmer in the eye of Awareness. More specifically, to "practice" time is to directly experience the source of the appearance of time, this very Awareness which is manifest as this timeless moment that never began.

112. The proper posture is that inner state which permits the uninterrupted contemplation of our true being. This is the real posture and not those physical postures that merely disturb our ease and happiness.

112. The benefits of the physical postures associated with Hatha Yoga are indisputable. But Shankara is not concerned with our short-lived bodies. His only concern is that we be acquainted with our true identity, with Reality.

The posture Shankara commends to us is an existential one. He encourages us to assume our position as the witness of the world, to acknowledge our most fundamental experience as this Awareness. We are That in which even space has its being.

113. The lauded first cause of all beings, the timeless support of the universe, in which enlightened beings are merged and immersed, this Being-Awareness is the real position, the true posture.

114. This nameless Reality, the root of all existence, is the only worthy object of meditation, the only sure means of restraining the mind. To bind the heart and mind to this ultimate and inconceivable One is to be rooted in the Ground of Being.

115. When the mind is fully absorbed in contemplation of this infinite Being that we are, the body and mind naturally fall into equilibrium. The mere straightening of the limbs is of little use.

116. One should learn to direct one's vision by recalling that the image of the world is Consciousness only and not what appears to the eye. This is called noble vision.

117. Or, let the vision be turned towards That in which the separation of the seer, the seeing, and the seen dissolves into unity. What good is staring at the tip of one's nose?

118. Learn to quiet all the disturbances in the mind by recognizing them as nothing but ripples in the ocean of Consciousness. All mental objects are Consciousness alone. Living in this Awareness is true control of the vital forces.

118. In verses 118 through 120 we find a short discussion of respiration and the vital force, a topic which, according to

Shankara's interpretation, is misunderstood by most spiritual aspirants. The vital force is known in Sanskrit as *prana*, a term which has already found its way into Western parlance. Prana is the vital energy, the life force that constitutes the physical aspect of being alive. It is the source of the vitality that is our health and our level of energy, truly, our vital force. While prana permeates the body, it is in the breath that it takes its subtle form and "breathes life" into the body. The volitional control of this vital force, this prana, is known by the Sanskrit word *pranayama*, which is also a commonplace term among practitioners of yoga throughout the world.

Yoga is an ancient science, a tradition composed of physical, mental, and spiritual practices designed to lead ultimately to union with God through the cessation of the modifications of the mind. The three major types of yoga are Karma Yoga, the yoga of action, of behavior, of cause and effect; Bhakti Yoga, the yoga of love and devotion; and Jnana Yoga, the yoga of knowledge and wisdom.

The practice of yoga, especially in the West, is misunderstood to be the performance of physical postures and breathing techniques along with periods of meditation which are, in many cases, exercises for developing concentration followed by periods of relaxation of the body and mind.

Since prana is usually associated with the breath, the practice of control of the vital forces in the West, and in many cases in the East, has gradually changed into an assortment of breathing exercises. Shankara, however, has an entirely different view of what it means to control the vital forces. Yoga, true yoga, he is telling us, is entirely spiritual.

119. True breath control is to see all as One. For those who insist upon breathing practices, let them discover the real breath. The real in-breath consists of holding the continuous thought, "I am this witnessing Awareness." The recognition of the unreality of all phenomena, including the body, the mind, and the universe is the aspect of breathing known as the real breathing out.

The Experience of Reality

120. Let the restraint of the breath be an opportunity to stabilize in the true Self as the source and totality of Being. This is the true method of breathing for the wise and not those popular breathing exercises that only torture the nose.

121. When everything that appears in the mind and senses is known to be the Self, we are practicing the true withdrawal of the senses. When the mind is merged in infinite Consciousness, all objects of perception disappear and the resplendent Self is revealed. This is the practice of the wise.

121. The Self alone is. Everything appears in, and as, this One Self. It follows then that there is nothing that can enter our realm of experience that is not fundamentally and finally this single Reality. This simple fact answers our questions and solves our problems, because everything is included, every contingency addressed. All the parts of our experience that seem to be other than the truth are, in fact, none other. Our fear and confusion, the suffering, ignorance and apparent evil we see in this world are not separate from the whole. Everything belongs. Everything appears and disappears in our lives and in our minds because of the Awareness that we are, because of the Being that we are.

Once we recognize this Awareness, this Self, as the source and ground of everything, the appearance of objects in our experience only *confirms* the Reality of this moment. This is the true withdrawal of the senses. When we rest in our basic identity as the Awareness in which everything appears, we are neither attracted to nor repulsed by the objects that appear. We abide as the timeless witness, beyond the pairs of opposites, beyond the mind altogether. We are simply Being. We *are* Being.

122. No matter how active the mind becomes, no matter where it wanders, true concentration is to recognize that Consciousness alone is the underlying reality, and all thoughts and all experiences, be they grave or glorious, are transient and relative. Realizing the truth of the Self, we hold steady in the knowledge that Awareness alone is real.

122. As concentration deepens and mental activity subsides, it becomes easier to apprehend this underlying presence, this infinite Awareness, that is the constant foundation of every object that arises. True concentration sees and feels a continuous atmosphere of totality and perfection, no matter what appears in the mind. This recognition brings the succession of objects of Awareness into sharper focus, helping us to appreciate both the quantity and quality of objects that appear in the Consciousness that we are.

As the mind becomes quiet, we may experience the kind of perceptions and feelings that are discussed in mystical literature. We may discover an expansion of our consciousness which brings a newfound clarity to the varied circumstances of our lives. We may feel an intimate relationship with other living beings and a powerful kinship and connection to every object, animate and inanimate.

As our understanding deepens, we recognize Awareness as the ground of all mental activity and thus as the source of all creatures and creation. We recognize also that this Awareness is the Being that we are. As objects appear in Awareness, we begin to see that everything that arises exists not only within us, but *as* us. Everything has its being in this Awareness that is the only Reality, and as we relax into being this one thing, we discover that we are everything.

123. We become independent of the movements of the mind through cultivating the unassailable thought, "I am none other than this pure witnessing Awareness." This is called meditation.

123. To become independent of the movements of the mind means that, though our normal thoughts are likely to

continue, albeit to a somewhat lesser degree, we are no longer confined by them. This is one of the keys to the true freedom that results from spiritual practice. Whether meditating or not, a stream of thoughts is the natural consequence of being in a human body. But if we recognize that the thoughts appearing in our minds are no different than birdsong or the noise of traffic, we are not tempted to follow our mental activity as if it were the primary focus and definition of our existence. When a thought arises that is relevant and useful, we notice that thought and respond to it according to the needs of the moment. But for the majority of thoughts that appear in our mind, we are free to let them be and to rest in the vastness of the Being-Awareness that is always here, prior to the appearance of each and every object. We listen to the stream of thoughts as though we are listening to the brook outside or a gentle rain on the roof, simply an inoffensive background noise that does not interfere with living the actual moment.

Shankara calls us to meditation for the best of reasons. Unlike the popular Western perception of meditation as a means to manage stress, lower blood pressure or cultivate peace of mind, Shankara presents us with both the meaning and the means of true meditation. The significance and the value of meditation is to provide a method by which we can answer the one question that includes all other questions: who am I?

In verse 123, we are given the means to answer this question. Happily, the means to answer the question is the answer to the question. Shankara says, in effect, 'I am not this face and these hands; I am not these thoughts and these feelings; I am truly nothing other than this pure witnessing Awareness.'

Many of us take up meditation and spiritual practice because it has become obvious that we are not experiencing the peace of mind that we know is available to us. Many of our lives are filled with unrest and confusion, angst and agitation, and our attempts to circumvent these disturbing elements have met with limited success. But we have heard of the existence and the possibility of something unlimited, so it seems only natural and prudent that we should respond to the ancient dictum: Know Thyself.

The human condition makes our identification with the body an inescapable consequence of *having* a body. True self-knowledge is not part of the natural course of a human life and only rarely happens spontaneously. For the rest of us, self-knowledge requires instruction and some degree of effort. Here, Shankara provides the instruction and gives us the tools to make the most intelligent use of our time and energy.

So we choose to meditate to "become independent of the movements of the mind." Notice that we are not told that the movements of the mind will stop, but we can become independent of the perpetual thought stream by recognizing our identity as That in which thoughts come and go. We can remind ourselves of this by employing Shankara's suggestion, "I am this pure witnessing Awareness," and by taking care to understand that this is not a sentence to be repeated, as if it were a mantra; it is a simple fact to be experienced. We steep ourselves in this knowledge, not by thinking about Awareness, but by being *this Awareness* that is attending to these words right now. This Awareness.

The mind may be busy or quiet, but our attention remains fixed upon our identity as this spacious presence in which everything happens. This is true meditation and infinitely more beneficial than conventional methods such as following the breath or repeating a sacred word or phrase. Authentic meditation is resting in, and as, this Awareness in which thoughts come and go. When we become established as this witnessing Awareness, thoughts subside without effort and the Self is revealed to be nothing other than this timeless presence, the Reality of this moment. Those who know this state speak of a subtle joy that permeates every part of their lives. Abiding as this Awareness reveals the ever-present bliss of Being.

124. Letting thought subside while holding onto the feeling that "There is only this Being-Awareness" leads to the dissolution of thought. We dissolve into changelessness and silence. This is known as absorption. It is also called real Knowledge.

124. As we come to the direct realization that all that finally exists in life is this Awareness, the thinking mind naturally begins to dissolve. Beyond all thought, beyond perception of any object, we are absorbed into Oneness.

In the yogic tradition, this is known as *samadhi*. It is popularly understood to be the final stage of spiritual attainment, but it is in actuality the inauguration of real spiritual life and heralds the advent of new dimensions of life for which words of description are inadequate and ultimately misleading.

As we arrive at the topic of samadhi, Shankara and Patanjali are in complete agreement. Samadhi is the eighth and final stage of Patanjali's Ashtanga path and the acknowledged goal for which all the foregoing stages of practice have been prescribed. "*Yoga citta vritti nirodh,*" says Patanjali. "Yoga is the cessation of mental activity in consciousness." The seven preliminary steps in Ashtanga yoga are all preparation for and prelude to this extraordinary phenomenon.

Samadhi, as suggested above, is not the end of the road. It has been stratified by advanced practitioners according to various stages that manifest within it. The most relevant distinction for our purposes, addresses whether there remains a sense of identity when we go beyond thought or whether we transcend all individuality, like a raindrop disappearing into the ocean. Although both of these aspects are defined as Samadhi, and even though the differences between them are exquisitely subtle, it is the total transcendence of all distinctions that marks complete absorption. We dissolve into the Reality of Being, beyond all identity.

While it is futile for the mind to attempt to construct concepts regarding absorption, it is not inaccurate for us to think of this dissolution of identity as transitioning from being to not-being. In fact, some of the world's great spiritual mentors declare that it is only when we cease to be that our true identity is revealed.

Once the mind falls silent and abides in this silence, there is nobody home; there is no I, there is no me, there is no "self," and *That* is the Self.

125. This best of practices should be undertaken regularly until, having become a natural part of one's life, it arises spontaneously and is always close at hand.

126. Once the Self is realized, the need for steps and practices falls away. We are what we are. Such a condition cannot be imagined. Who can describe Being?

127. The practice of silence and self-knowledge is likely to be hampered by obstacles. Among the most common difficulties are idleness, boredom, pointless thoughts not devoted to the holy ideal, and the desire for sensory enjoyment.

127. In this and the next verse, Shankara enumerates our old friends, the obstacles. But we have already learned that, even in those moments when we may feel beset by these obstacles, we are simply the *awareness* of these obstacles. We are neither their cause nor their victim. Everything depends upon what we take ourselves to be.

128. Other obstacles to absorption in the Self are lack of concentration, distraction by pleasures and pains, paralysis of the intellect, fatigue and sleep, to name a few. Each of these distractions must be met as it arises. The fruitfulness of our practice depends upon how we relate to these diversions.

The Experience of Reality

129. When the mind focuses upon an object, that object fills the mind. By thinking of the void, the mind becomes objectless and empty. When the mind is fixed upon The Absolute, the mind will be filled with the glory of the transcendental Spirit that manifests as all the universes. Therefore, we should constantly think of that One which is beyond thought until there is only One.

129. We have all heard it said, "As we think, so we become." In the *Aparokshanubhuti*, Shankara encourages us to think on that which is beyond the body and beyond even the mind. It will not do to cultivate a simple blankness of mind, for such a state is little different from stupor. By pointing the mind toward the emptiness of the void, we are gazing into the unfathomable fullness of the Absolute which naturally contains the void and is infinitely beyond even the dualism of being and not-being.

To attempt to think of the Absolute requires that we dispense with thought altogether, for thought obscures Truth which can only be revealed in the spacious presence beyond the mind. So Shankara says we should constantly think of the Absolute and goes on the say that we can only do this by ceasing to think. When thinking ceases, only Being remains. Recall the words, "We should constantly think of that One which is beyond thought until there is only One." When thoughts vanish, we vanish with them, and all that remains is what always is. Immediately and timelessly, we are who we truly are

130. Those of us who do not center our lives around the holy truth surely live in vain. Though we may exist like other living beings, if we are oblivious to our reason for being, we have squandered this precious incarnation.

131. Blessed are those wise ones who heed the call of Truth and taste Reality. They are worthy of praise and are sure to grow in completeness and joy.

132. There are some among us who have embraced this Knowledge so completely that they have been absorbed into the supreme Spirit even while they live. They are not to be confused with those who merely talk about the supreme state but do not strive to attain it.

132. The recommendation here is that we strive to attain this supreme state. The striving that is required, however, is so subtle that the word barely applies. The real challenge is in recognizing which knowledge is the true Knowledge and then applying this Knowledge in life.

There are so many kinds of "spiritual" knowledge available that it is difficult to distinguish which kinds of knowledge we should pursue. This is a natural source of confusion because *all* genuine spiritual teachings are beneficial and relatively true. How are we to discriminate between the absolute Knowledge that Shankara commends and the more dualistic knowledge common to traditional religious and spiritual teaching? This is where the striving should commence. This is also a theme of Shankara'a most well-known writing, *The Crest Jewel of Discrimination.*

For Shankara, discrimination is the means by which we differentiate between the real and the unreal, the actual and the apparent, the timeless and the transient. The teachings that constitute real Knowledge are the last to be applied, because upon comprehension of this precious information, there are no more questions, no unused pieces of the puzzle.

Some of us passionately anchor on a set of ideas about spiritual knowledge before we have absorbed it in its entirety. We can periodically validate this knowledge by examining the frequency and content of our mental activity. We can drop a pebble of doubt into the ocean of infinite Being and watch to see if there are any ripples. When the mind is still, doubts disappear.

The Experience of Reality

133. Many of us are skillful in speaking about the Holy Spirit, but we have no direct experience to enliven our message. We have not undertaken true spiritual practice and we remain entangled in the affairs of the world. We inflict our ignorance upon others and actively perpetuate our own separation from the very God we profess to represent.

133. Hearing and reading and thinking and talking about the ultimate mystery are poor substitutes for the direct experience of Reality which Shankara urges upon us.

134. The true aspirant does not allow a single mental moment to pass that does not hold the Absolute as both the background and centerpiece of every experience. Each moment arises within this holy framework.

135. The cause may be reflected in the effect, but the effect can never illuminate the real cause. The entire universe is merely an effect and eventually is recognized as unreal. When the mind is brought to stillness by deep contemplation, all phenomena cease to exist. The effect disappears and, with it, the imagined cause. In this way we realize That which is Absolute, nondual, beyond the causal principle, beyond the realm of things, pure Existence, pure Intelligence; Bliss.

136. Thus we find ourselves in that state in which all distinction and separation has dissolved into the causeless and relationless One. Here we find no place for words or thought. Remember the illustration of the earth that makes up every sort of pottery. So does everything that appears to be, exist in name only. In Truth, there is only the nameless Absolute.

137. Practicing in this way, cultivating stillness and discriminating between the real and the impermanent, there dawns in the mind the recognition of our identity as the infinite Self. Then we know the pure-minded state of Awareness and enjoy supreme happiness.

138. We can develop greater clarity by seeing all things in the universe as the effects of a single cause, the Absolute, the One. Then we discern the existence of this One Self everywhere, inherent in every phenomenon, in each living being, and every drop of water.

139. Thus is the cause seen in every effect. As the mind returns to stillness, the individual effects dissolve into that stillness. As the effects disappear, so does the cause cease to have meaning. In this way we transcend the causal relationship and remain as That which is nondual and prior to everything: Being, Consciousness, Bliss.

140. Our true nature is divine. It is only our inability to accept our inherent divinity that perpetuates the illusion of a separate individual. If we allow ourselves to embrace the holy teachings as truth and meditate upon this Oneness, we find ourselves to be the Truth. If we were to cultivate the unshakable conviction that we truly are the divine Being described in the holy scriptures, we would realize this Reality which we already are.

141. This whole world, visible and invisible, is born entirely of Consciousness. By virtue of our own experience, our own undeniable Existence, our meditation will lead us to confess, "I am this Awareness."

The Experience of Reality

141. Eventually, the obvious becomes obvious: we are. This being that we are in this moment is absolute Being. There are no spiritual practices that can bring Being into existence. It is this very presence that we always are; it is our essence, our default mode. This most basic of facts can burst upon us in the form of a revelation, or dawn in us so gradually that we do not notice that we have shifted from our habitual reactions to life to a simple witnessing, free from judgment and commentary. We may only become aware of this change when it is pointed out to us by others who have noticed that we seem to be more easy-going and more open-minded. Shankara's words are carefully chosen to lead us to this subtle but readily apparent truth: everything arises within this Being-Awareness that is, and can only be, who we are. Everything exists in, and because of, Awareness.

As we become established in this immediate Presence in which everything happens, we gradually lose even our sense of identity as the knower of the field of existence. We no longer experience ourselves as separate from anything that arises. We no longer experience ourselves, period. There is only what is.

142. We should look upon every object of perception as a simple manifestation of Consciousness. Thereby we come to know that each and every thing that appears before us is Consciousness alone. Thus are we freed from the tyranny of appearances, and thus do we come to live in the freedom and felicity of the natural state, resting in the bliss of pure Awareness, the true Self.

142. The great truth of nonduality is that there is only One. Being and nothingness do not comprise the One, but are merely conceptual constituents of the Absolute, about which nothing can be said or thought. Yet, our appreciation of the meaning of this Oneness, leaves us exactly where Shankara wants us to be. If there is only One, then everything is it. If everything is the same thing, then, undeniably and inescapably, we must be this One. If we are able to come to terms with this inexpressibly profound and simple truth, we will realize that every moment of our lives is nothing other than the experience of Reality.

Coming from the depths of this realization, life begins to live itself without our intervention. We simply watch ourselves and our world happen, instinctively, automatically. We become so much a part of everything that, ultimately, even the witness disappears. Our consciousness of our individuality vanishes into the actuality of what is, for there is no longer any separation; no one who is conscious and no object of which to be conscious; there is only This. The experience of Reality merges into Reality and we are nowhere to be found.

143. These fifteen steps of spiritual practice herein described comprise the true royal path to realization of absolute Truth and the freedom that attends it. These steps are not to be confused with those lesser practices which occupy the energies of most aspirants. These steps may be combined with more physical routines for those who are not fully prepared for the demands of committed spiritual practice.

143. So what began as a search for the experience of Reality reveals that there is no such thing as the experience of Reality, because there is only One. The dualities of seeker and sought, of seer and seen, dissolve into what always, already is. Even our notions of Reality and Oneness disappear. There is only This; pure, perfect, complete.

144. Those whose minds and hearts are ripe for this great Knowledge, and who are earnest and devoted to the highest good, will find this a most accessible and productive method for realizing the ultimate Truth of life.

Afterword

Aparokshanubhuti was written specifically for our benefit. Here we have been exposed to some of the most outspoken and straightforward spiritual instruction available in any language, from any era of our history. Shankara assures us that liberation is possible in this very lifetime. Liberation means freedom from ignorance. Ignorance, he tells us, is not knowing who and what we really are, and from this primary misapprehension spring all other forms of ignorance.

Ignorance is a natural product of the human condition. None of us can escape the initial conviction that we are an individual human body living a discrete and limited life. Some fortunate few among us may intuit a deeper truth early on, but for most of us, there are years of searching and struggle in store for us before we recognize the deathless nature of our true Being.

In recent decades, many people have begun to distill the teachings sufficiently to shorten the process of awakening by learning to avoid the quagmire of concepts, the thinking mind, the very source of the confusion that leads to perpetual seeking. Little did we know that what we were looking for, the only true thing, is our own inescapable Being, standing so close to us that we did not notice it; so very close, in fact, that we *are* It.

Shankara strikes at the principal ignorance that keeps us bound to the finite world. Again and again he says, "You are not the body." He goes on to present a host of reasons why we are steeped in misunderstanding, all the while repeatedly insisting that we are not, nor have we ever been, so limited as we have imagined ourselves to be.

Shankara does not simply tell us what we are not; he also tells us what and who we are: "You are the Self; You are Supreme Spirit, the transcendental Reality." Surely, it is intriguing to hear words like this, but it is quite another thing to know beyond doubt that such an imposing statement is perfectly true and not just another platitude. We may be told that honey is sweet and exquisitely delicious, but until we have tasted it for ourselves, the taste of honey is only hearsay and imagination. There can be no proof of our true identity except to experience it directly.

109

The Experience of Reality

Nothing else will do. It is for this reason that Shankara gives us the fifteen steps, so that we may taste for ourselves.

Beginning at verse 100, the fifteen steps are introduced and delineated in conjunction with an examination and comparison of the eight steps of Patanjali's Ashtanga Yoga which was the conventional yogic practice of Shankara's era and remains so today. Shankara suggests alternative interpretations of Patanjali's practices with what amounts to the same course of action that he proposes in each of his fifteen steps. It turns out that Shankara's fifteen steps are a bit of a ruse, for each and every step he prescribes for us recommends only one thing, the same thing, every time.

Here, in review, are a few examples of Shankara's fifteen 'different' steps:

- Constantly hold the conviction that 'All of this is God and nothing else.'
- Cultivate and perpetuate a unitive thought such as "All is One," to the exclusion of all other kinds of thought.
- See every object of perception as Awareness alone.
- Even when speaking, the wise should always strive to be one with that Great Silence from which words, together with the mind, turn back.
- By the practice of place is meant abidance in the solitude of pure space.
- The proper posture is that inner state which permits the uninterrupted contemplation of our true Being.
- Let the restraint of the breath be an opportunity to stabilize in the true Self as the source and totality of Being.
- We become independent of the movements of the mind through cultivating the unassailable thought, "I am none other than this pure witnessing Awareness."
- We should constantly think of that One which is beyond thought until there is only One.

Afterword

Finally, there is only one thing to be done, and for that we have no adequate words. Perhaps as close as we can come is to actively and energetically take on the most challenging of practices: Be! This is to say, do nothing, and watch carefully.

There is nothing we can "do" to bring about the experience of Reality. Reality is, in every moment, front and center in our lives. It is only our inadvertence, our ignorance, our belief in the contents of the thinking mind, that obscures the truth of our infinite Being which is ever-present; the very definition of here and now. Ignorance is born of, composed of, and perpetuated by thought. When thought ceases, ignorance ceases; the clouds disappear and Reality remains, resplendent.

When considering Reality, any thought is an erroneous thought. Mental activity in the form of ideas and concepts can be useful for helping us determine what is not true, but when we turn toward absolute Truth, thoughts can only obscure the purity of what always, already is. There are, in fact, no true ideas, no ultimate views. We can know what is not; what is, we can only Be; and this is our task. This is the practice: Being.

Why should it be so difficult to be what we already are? It is impossible to truly be anything else, and yet we struggle so to become it. What is going on here? Simply put, *We* are going on here; and Shankara, in accord with the great wisdom traditions, is imploring us to stop going on. Stop searching, stop wanting, stop seeking. Stop. Be still.

Ultimately, this is all that is required of us. It is the culmination of all spiritual paths and the essence of Shankara's instruction. Be still. In stillness our true Being is revealed. Initially, our silence may last for only a second or two at a time, but if we are earnest and devoted, the seconds will grow into moments and the moments into timelessness. Eventually, it will not matter if thoughts are present or not, for the underlying stillness, the light of Being, will shine out of every moment and pervade all forms of manifestation. Then, wherever we look, we will see only One and know that it is only the One seeing itself. All One.

A new journey begins here. Just as the attainment of samadhi seemed to be the grand finale, but proved to be only the beginning of a more profound journey, so do we now embark on an even greater adventure. As our life in the world continues, we grow into ever

The Experience of Reality

deeper dimensions of the experience of Reality until we come upon the unspeakable miracle of Love and discover the very Source of Being and Not-Being, the crucible of the Universes. Unexpectedly, we realize that the source of the impersonal and formless One is not a void; It is none other than the nameless and glorious Heart of Reality, beyond all realms, beyond all terms.

Having realized the truth of our Being, we grow into ever greater awareness of the infinite Love that is the core and substance of all aspects of existence, from the atom to the Absolute. We also instantly know that every fellow human Being in this wide world is, and can only be, this One Being. Each and every one of us is a complete and perfect manifestation of the light of Reality, whether we know it or not. And here begins this next adventure: *expressing* the radiance of Being.

Once we have uncovered the glories of Being, we still find ourselves living in this relative world. So how shall we proceed? We would be within our rights to simply remain undisturbed, content to bask in the bliss of Existence. It has been said that those who are awakened and who remain stationary, have a profound impact on their surroundings. But once we have discovered this most precious Knowledge, does it seem a little selfish to keep it to ourselves? There must be something we can do.

We have ample evidence that shouting from the rooftops is rarely helpful, and, more than anything, we want to help. So how to go about it? First, let's be still. Each of us has different qualities, different gifts. We may not have the cure for cancer or the recipe for world peace, but it is certain that no one else can play our part. Nor need we even know what that part is, except in the playing of it. We breathe in, we breathe out, we live this moment as the Being that we are, and everything happens by itself.

As we dissolve into this infinite Being, we are compelled by Love to make a contribution to this life that we share with our neighbors. Our role may evolve into leadership, but for many of us, our greatest gift will be the example we are, the Presence that we bring to each moment of life as this Awareness radiates out into the world from far beyond us. As we dissolve into this Oneness, we will be what we are. As we disappear into this Love, we will know what to do.

May we be so permeated by this revelation that we come to live this timeless moment from the depths of our natural condition:
This infinite Being, the totality of *this* moment... right now.

Acknowledgements

Profound gratitude to Sri Shankaracharya and all who have tasted Reality and attempted to communicate it to us.

We can do nothing by ourselves.
Deepest thanks to Edmund and Florence Kloss, Christina Laurel, Ian Kloss, Ted Perry, John VanLare, Corey Vance, Richard Trowbridge and Robert Carwithen.

Appendix A

Publications Relating to the Introduction

- Advaita of Shankara, S.G. Modgal
- Advaita Vedanta: A Philosophical Reconstruction, Eliot Deutsch
- *Advaitic Mysticism of Shankara*, A. Ramamurti
- *Agricultural and Pastoral Societies in Ancient and Classical History*, Michael Adas
- *Ancient Cities of the Indus Valley Civilization*, Jonathan Mark Kenoyer
- *Ancient Indian Economic Thought, Relevance for Today*, Ratan Lal Basu & Rajkumar Sen:
- *The Ancient Indus: Urbanism, Economy, and Society*, Rita P. Wright
- *The Ancient South Asian World*, Jonathan Mark Kenoyer
- *The Archaeology of Early Historic South Asia: The Emergence of Cities and States*, Raymond Allchin
- *The Cambridge Economic History of India: Volume 2*, Dharma Kumar, Desai Meghnad, eds.
- *The Earliest Civilization of South Asia*, B.B. Lal
- *Encyclopedia of Indian Philosophies*, Karl H. Potter, ed.
- *Essays on Ancient India*, Raj Kumar
- *Excavations at Harappa*, M.S. Vats
- *Finding Forgotten Cities*, Nayanjot Lahiri
- *Forgotten Cities on the Indus*, Michael Jansen, Marie Mulloy, eds.
- *Further Excavations at Mohenjo-Daro*, E.J.H. Mackay
- *Geometry in Ancient and Medieval India*, Saraswati Amma
- *Harappa Excavations 1986 – 1990: A Multidisciplinary Approach to Third Millennium Urbanism*, Richard Meadow, ed.
- *A History of Ancient and Early Medieval India: From the Stone Age to the 12th Century*, Upinder Singh
- *History of Hindu Mathematics*, B.B. Dutta

- *History of Humanity, Volume III, From the Third Millennium to the Seventh Century BC*, Ahmad Hassan Dani, J-P Mohen. eds.
- *The History of Mathematics: An Introduction*, David M. Burton
- *The History of Mathematics: A Brief Course*, Roger Cooke
- *India 1947-1997: New Light on the Indus Civilization*, B.B. Lal
- *The Indus Civilization: A Contemporary Perspective*, Gregory Possehl
- *In Search of the Cradle of Civilization*, Georg Feuerstein
- *Introduction to Advaita Vedanta*, Krishnan Ayyar
- *Life in the Ancient Indus River Valley*, Hazel Richardson
- *Mohenjo-daro and the Indus Civilization*, John Marshall, ed.
- *Origins of a Civilization: The Prehistory and Early Archaeology of South Asia*, Bridget Allchi
- *A Peaceful Realm: The Rise and Fall of the Indus Civilization*, Jane McIntosh
- *People of the Earth: An Introduction to World Prehistory*, Brian Fagan
- *The Quest for the Origins of Vedic Culture*, Edwin Bryant
- *The Rise of Civilization in India and Pakistan*, Bridget Allchin
- *A Samkara Source-book*, A.J.Alston
- *Shankara and Indian Philosophy*, N.V. Isaeva
- Shankara's Advaita, Raghunath D. Karmarkar
- *A Short History of Pakistan*, A.H. Dani
- *South Asian Archaeology 1989*, Catharine Jarrige, ed.
- *The Universal History of Numbers: From prehistory to the Invention of the Computer*, Georges Ifrah
- *World History: Patterns of Interaction*, Roger B. Beck, Linda Black, Phillip Naylor, Dahia Ibo Shabaka
- *The Wonder That Was India*, A.L. Basham
- *The Yoga Tradition: It's History, Literature, Philosophy and Practice*, Georg Feuerstein

118

Related Websites

- advaita-vedanta.org
- adventurecorps.com
- ancienthistory.about.com
- ancientindia.com.uk
- ancientscripts.com
- ancientwisdom.com.uk
- archaeologyonline.net
- art-and-archaeology.com
- atimes.com
- bbc.co.uk
- Britannica.com
- Bronze.uco.edu
- crystallinks.com
- culturalindia.net
- csuchico.edu
- facts-about-india.com
- freeindia.org
- gap-system.org
- harappa.com
- harvard.academia.edu
- historia.net
- history-world.org
- iloveindia.com
- indhistory.com
- india.gov.in
- indiaonline.in
- indiasite.com
- indianetzone.com
- indus-civilization.info
- indusvalleycivilizatio n.webs.com
- kamakoti.org
- library.think-quest.org
- mahavidya.ca
- mohenjodaro.net
- onlinelibrary.wiley.com
- sankaracharya.org
- Sanskrit.org
- sscnet.ucla.edu
- swamiji.com
- thisismyindia.com
- vedicsciences.net
- webindia123.com
- wikipedia.org

Appendix B

Source Texts

APAROKSHANUBHUTI
or Self Realiization of Sri Shankaracharya
Text, with word-for-word translation, English Rendering
and Notes By Swami Vimuktananda

DIRECT EXPERIENCE OF REALITY
Verses from the Aparokshanubhuti of Shri Shankaracharya
Translated with a Commentary by Hari Prasad Shastri

APAROKSANUBHUTI
Intimate Experience of the Reality By Sri Adi Sankaracarya
Commentary by Swami Chinmayananda

DIRECT EXPERIENCE OF "I-AM"
Aparokshanubhuti by Shri Shankaracharya
Translated and Commentary by Shri Brahmananda Sarasvati

DIRECT AWARENESS OF THE SELF
A Translation of the APAROKSANUBHUTI by Sankara
Translated, with historical introduction and commentary by
Douglas A. Fox

DIRECT COGNITION OF THE UNITY OF JIVA AND
BRAHMA
By Srimat Sankaracharya with notes Translated by
Manilal Nabubhai Dvivedi

APARAKSHANUBHOOTHI
(Non indirect experience)
A philosophic treatise on Advaitha by
Adhishankara Bhagwat Pada
Transliteration and translation by P.R. Ramachander